OUR HOLY FAITH
A RELIGION SERIES for THE ELEMENTARY SCHOOLS

TEACHER'S MANUAL for

God's Truths Help Us Live

Based on the first half of the
No. 1 Revised Baltimore Catechism
(Confraternity Edition)

ST. AUGUSTINE ACADEMY PRESS
HOMER GLEN, ILLINOIS

Nihil obstat:
: JOHN A. SCHULIEN
: Censor librorum

Imprimatur:
: + GULIELMUS E. COUSINS
: Archiepiscopus Milwauchiensis
: May 20, 1959

This book was originally published in 1959 by Bruce Publishing, Milwaukee.

This reprinted edition ©2017 by St. Augustine Academy Press
ISBN: 978-1-64051-015-9

CONTENTS

General Introduction for the Series "Our Holy Faith" . 5

Unit One. We Belong to God 9
    I. Introduction to Unit One 9
    II. Work Study Periods for Unit One . . . 10
    III. Culmination of Unit One 19
    IV. Evaluation of Unit One 19

Unit Two. Who and What God Is 22
    I. Introduction to Unit Two 22
    II. Work Study Periods for Unit Two . . . 23
    III. Culmination of Unit Two 35
    IV. Evaluation of Unit Two 35

Unit Three. God the Son Became Man to Save Us . 37
    I. Introduction to Unit Three 37
    II. Work Study Periods for Unit Three . . 37
    III. Culmination of Unit Three 46
    IV. Evaluation of Unit Three 46

Unit Four. Jesus Dies for Us 48
    I. Introduction to Unit Four 48
    II. Work Study Periods for Unit Four . . 48
    III. Culmination of Unit Four 56
    IV. Evaluation of Unit Four 57

Unit Five. God the Holy Ghost Comes to Do His Work   59

    I. Introduction to Unit Five 59

    II. Work Study Periods for Unit Five . . . 59

    III. Culmination of Unit Five 66

    IV. Evaluation of Unit Five 67

Unit Six. The Work of the Holy Ghost in the Church   68

    I. Introduction to Unit Six 68

    II. Work Study Periods for Unit Six . . . 68

    III. Culmination of Unit Six 76

    IV. Evaluation of Unit Six 76

Unit Seven. How We Love and Serve God   . . 78

    I. Introduction to Unit Seven 78

    II. Work Study Periods for Unit Seven . . 78

    III. Culmination of Unit Seven 86

    IV. Evaluation of Unit Seven 86

GENERAL INTRODUCTION FOR THE SERIES

OUR HOLY FAITH

The Series, OUR HOLY FAITH, is intended to provide a complete, integrated, and basic course in religion for the eight grades of the elementary school.

The purpose of teaching religion in the elementary school is to see to it that the pupil has a clear and adequate knowledge of his holy Faith, so as to guide and influence his will to use grace in forming the image of Christ in himself. While primarily addressed to the intellect, it does not neglect the will or the child's attitudes and emotions. The first purpose of this religion Series, therefore, is clear and adequate knowledge of the Catholic religion.

The psychological basis for this is to be found in St. Augustine's little gem, "On Catechizing the Unlettered."*

St. Augustine tells us that in teaching religion we must lead the pupil from faith, to hope, to charity. The first step, therefore, is knowledge of our religion based on supernatural faith. The child is taught and accepts what Christ's Church, through her representative, proposes to be believed.

Content and Arrangement of the Series — Grades 1 and 2

The content of the first two grades is the traditional content of those grades, with emphasis on Confession and Holy Communion in the second grade.

Grades 3, 4, and 5

The first two grades are followed by two cycles of three grades each — 3 to 5 and 6 to 8. In Grades 3, 4, and 5, the No. 1 Baltimore Catechism is followed in the exact sequence of its lessons and indeed of its questions, in such fashion, however, that the first half of the No. 1 Revised Baltimore Catechism** (the Creed and the first three Commandments) is covered in the first book of that sequence (GOD'S TRUTHS HELP US LIVE); the second half of the No. 1 Catechism is covered in the third book of that sequence (OUR FAITH: GOD'S GREAT GIFT). The second book of that sequence (THE VINE AND THE BRANCHES) is devoted to a study of the liturgy and the liturgical year. In this book the catechetical approach is, for obvious reasons, omitted. We have placed this material, which deals with an important area of religious instruction omitted in the Catechism, between two books devoted to explaining the Catechism.

Thus, the suggested sequence for Grades 3 to 5 is:

Grade 3 — GOD'S TRUTHS HELP US LIVE
(First half of No. 1 Catechism)

Grade 4 — THE VINE AND THE BRANCHES
(The liturgy and the liturgical year)

Grade 5 — LIVING LIKE CHRIST IN CHRIST
(Second half of No. 1 Catechism)

One value of this sequence is that it provides an alternation from the Catechism, applying the same doctrines but in a completely different manner.

Grades 6, 7, and 8

The books for the three remaining grades — 6, 7, and 8 — are similarly organized. In the first book of the sequence, OUR FAITH: GOD'S GREAT GIFT, the pupil studies the first half of the No. 2 Revised Baltimore Catechism. The second half of the No. 2 Catechism is then taken up in the volume, TO LIVE IS CHRIST, which is recommended for Grade 8 because it contains a review of the first half of the No. 2 Catechism and an intense study of its second half. The third book in this sequence (recommended for Grade 7, but usable in any grade from the sixth to the eighth) is entitled CHRIST: IN PROPHECY, IN PERSON, AND IN HIS CHURCH. It contains a complete chronological treatment of Bible History and of Church History, which have often been neglected in recent courses of study. The suggested sequence for Grades 6 to 8 is this:

Grade 6 — OUR FAITH: GOD'S GREAT GIFT
(First half of No. 2 Catechism)

Grade 7 — CHRIST: IN PROPHECY, IN PERSON, AND IN HIS CHURCH
(Bible History — Church History)

Grade 8 — TO LIVE IS CHRIST
(Second half of No. 2 Catechism)

Flexibility of the Series

Although the Series follows the sequence of the Catechism, its subject matter is so arranged that it is pos-

---

* There are many translations; that of Rev. Joseph P. Christopher, *De catechizandis Rudibus* (Washington, D. C.: Catholic University, 1926), is very good.

** All references to the Catechism are to the Confraternity Edition.

sible for a superintendent, a pastor, or a principal to adapt it to almost every course of study for religion in the elementary grades, or vice versa, to adapt the course of study to fit the Series. Since it contains books that are devoted to a study of the liturgy and of biblical and Church history, the Series makes it possible for the teacher to break up the monotony that frequently results from studying nothing but the Catechism year after year.

It is suggested that the book covering the first half of the No. 1 Catechism be used in Grade 3 and that the one dealing with the second half be employed for Grade 5, with the book on the liturgy for Grade 4. However the order of sequence can be changed if another order seems more appropriate. The book on the liturgy, THE VINE AND THE BRANCHES, can be postponed to Grade 5 if it is thought too difficult for Grade 4 (it is, however, no more difficult than science or geography in that grade); or it can be anticipated in an earlier grade or even completely omitted. The latter possibility, however, is one which the authors hope is not considered. Our present courses of study in elementary religion almost universally omit an ordered and intensive study of the liturgy and the liturgical year, which, as Pope Pius XII reminded us, is a basic means of religious instruction.

Method of Handling the Catechism

In the past, the method of teaching religion in the elementary schools was, quite justly, criticized for its misuse of the Catechism. The fault certainly did not lie in the Catechism which is intended as a concise and precise synopsis of religious knowledge. The Catechism is designed to be studied carefully *after* it has been taught and explained authoritatively in the name of the Church.

Too often, however, the authoritative teaching and presentation has been omitted, and the child has been led directly to the bald, synoptic questions and answers of the Catechism, which he has been directed to study before or without any explanation and then repeat in rote fashion after he has memorized them.

Fortunately, in most modern courses of study in religion this abuse has been eliminated. The result has been courses of study more enjoyable to teacher and pupil alike.

Unfortunately, in many instances, the Catechism has also been abandoned. Bishops and pastors have deplored this, with great justification. An ordered knowledge of one's religion is absolutely necessary, and this the Catechism insures.

In this Series we have retained the exact sequence of the Catechisms No. 1 and No. 2. However, we have taken care to teach the content of the lessons *before* asking the child to study and, if needed, to memorize the Catechism questions and answers. Thus we hope we have met the reasonable desires of the clergy, by accenting the Catechism, while not forgetting the needs and problems of the pupils and teachers in the classroom.

In many instances, while following the Catechism, we have added points not covered in it, but necessary either as matters of knowledge or as material aiding assimilation and application of the basic doctrines. Our intention has been to make the study of religion as attractive and enjoyable and instructive as possible. In short, we believe that a child's attitude toward religion is as important as his knowledge. One without the other is not of much value, and in this Series we have sought to integrate the two.

In this connection, however, let it be clearly stated and understood that the child's inclination or enjoyment is not the prime factor to be considered. We are dealing here with a matter that is not subject to the likes or dislikes of the pupil. Here we are concerned with a divinely constituted body of knowledge which the Church has a mandate to convey to the human race, and particularly to her members, in an authoritative way. "As the Father hath sent me, I also send you. Going therefore . . ." (Mt. 28:28).

Here, a curriculum solely determined by child interest or enjoyment would be an absurdity.

A Key Point — The Answer Before the Question

In the four years in which the texts of the Series are based directly on the Catechism — Grades 3, 5, 6, and 8 — we have included the Catechism answers in the body of the lessons, using the exact words of the Catechism; but we have expanded, paraphrased, and otherwise explained the meaning of the Catechism; this will insure that the child understands what the Catechism means, and will assist him to learn it when he studies the Catechism questions and answers at the end of the lesson. *The Catechism answers have been placed in boldface or in italics* to call attention to them. Thus, we teach the answer before we ask the child to learn it. The result is *understanding,* not mere rote memorization.

BASIC PRINCIPLES IN TEACHING RELIGION

What follows are the essential and fundamental principles for the teaching of religion. All else is accidental.

Begin With Faith

The first objective of the teaching of religion is a knowledge of the truths God wants us to know, and an acceptance of those truths on the basis of God's veracity — namely, an informed but unhesitating faith.

End With Love

The supreme objective of the teaching of religion, however, is not faith but love — love of God. The objective we have had in building this Series, and the objective the teachers of religion must have in teaching it, is to lead the pupil to a supernatural love of God.

With St. Augustine we ask every teacher of this Series to refer everything she teaches to the love of

God — God's love for us as proved by what He has done for us, and our love of God as proved by how we serve God in Himself and in our neighbors.

With God's love for us and ours for Him ever in mind, the teacher should present the doctrines and moral precepts of the Catholic religion in such a fashion that they lead the child first to an appreciation of his faith and a strengthening of that virtue in him; then to an increase of hope in him, for without supernatural hope there will be no continued striving.

The end, however, is love. The pupil should be led to see in everything that God has done an evidence of His love for us. He has loved us enough to reveal to us what He wants us to believe. He has revealed His existence, the incarnation, the redemption, the Church, the sacraments, the moral code we follow, the rewards He has in store for us, and so many other matters. In each of these truths He is proving His love for us. They should be so taught that, in all, God's love of us may stand out and arouse a desire to return love for love.

If truths are so taught, it will be easy for the child to see his obligation to love and serve God in return. They will not then be merely abstract truths with little personal meaning, but will become knowledge charged with motives for the will to require that divine love.

Method and Content Intertwined

From the above it will be seen that method and content in the proper teaching of religion are closely intertwined. The point to be learned is first presented to the intellect as an object of faith and knowledge, then related to hope, as being possible, and finally to love as being something to be desired and possessed. All other details of methodology should be subordinated to this basic sequence.

It is all the more necessary to insist on this because the unit method we have used is also commonly employed in teaching the social studies. There, however, it is not based on supernatural virtues, but on the natural intellectual virtues.

Christian Formation

The formation of the perfect Christian, whose life is patterned on the life of Christ, is our final goal. This cannot be achieved by teaching or by the school. It is a supernatural task, requiring supernatural means. These means are in the possession of the Church. All the teacher can do is instruct and influence the pupil to fulfill his destiny as a member of Christ's Mystical Body, to see his role in the sacrifice it offers to the heavenly Father, to utilize the channels of grace it offers him. Solid, accurate, and full instruction by the teacher means much, but it does not guarantee the co-operation of the student. He still has his free will. The teacher can instruct, give good example, and pray — in doing these she does much. The home, too, can do much. But the grace of God, the Church and her means of grace, and the free will of the individual are all-important. We must do our utmost to enlighten the intellect and train the will of our charges — then leave the rest to God.

PUPILS' GENERAL OBJECTIVES FOR THE YEAR

A. To gain such an understanding of the chief truths of the Catholic Faith found in the Apostles' Creed that these truths may serve as motives for Christian virtue.
B. To learn that the Mass continues the Sacrifice of the Cross, and to learn to assist at it with devotion.
C. To gain a knowledge of the commandments as a means of loving and serving God.
D. To gain a simple knowledge of and interest in the liturgical life of the Church.
E. To develop an attitude of dependence on God in all things.
F. To further the understanding and appreciation of the infinite price paid by Christ for our redemption.
G. To awaken a desire to share more fully in the divine life of grace.
H. To co-operate with grace in developing the virtues of faith, hope, and love.
I. To strive to be a worthy member of Christ's Mystical Body by daily living with Christ and by promoting the kingdom of Christ through good example.
J. To form Christian characters by applying the religious knowledge acquired in living in and with Christ in the seasons and feasts of the liturgical year.

GENERAL REFERENCES FOR THE TEACHER
(Starred texts strongly recommended)

*1. Baierl, Rev. Joseph, *The Creed Explained* (St. Paul.: Catechetical Guild).
*2. Baierl, Rev. Joseph, *The Commandments Explained* (St. Paul: Catechetical Guild).
*3. Belger, Sister Josita, C.S.F., *Sing a Song of Holy Things* (Milwaukee: The Tower Press).
*4. Holy Bible (Paterson, N. J.: St. Anthony Guild Press).
*5. Thayer, Mary Dixon, *The Child on His Knees* (New York: Macmillan Co.).
6. LeBuffe, Rev. Francis P., S.J., *Let's Try Mental Prayer* (St. Louis: The Queen's Work).
7. Brennan, Rev. Gerald T., *Angel Food Series* (Milwaukee: Bruce).
8. Christopher and Spence, *The Raccolta* (New York: Benziger Bros.).
9. Dennerle, Rev. George, *Leading the Little Ones to Christ* (Milwaukee: Bruce).
10. Dorcy, Sister Jean, O.P., *Mary My Mother* (New York: Sheed & Ward).
11. Fuerst, Rev. A. N., *The Systematic Teaching of Religion* (Chicago: Benziger).
12. Hannon, Rev. J. D., *Teacher Tells a Story*, Vols. I & II (Chicago: Benziger).
13. Hosty, Rev. Thomas, *Small Talks for Small People* (Milwaukee: Bruce).
14. Johnson, Rev. George, *The Bible Story* (New York: Benziger Bros.).
15. Kelly, Most Rev. Edward J., D.D., *Baltimore Catechism No. 1 With Development* (Boise, Idaho: The Chancery Office, Box 769).

16. Lord, Rev. D., S.J., *Miniature Stories of the Saints*, Vols. I & II (New York: Wm. J. Hirter Co., Inc.).
17. Lovasik, Rev. Lawrence, *Catechism Sketched* (St. Paul: Catechetical Guild).
18. Marguerite, Sister Mary, *Their Hearts Are His Garden* (Paterson, N. J.: St. Anthony Guild Press).
19. Mary, Sister, *The Catholic Mother's Helper* (Paterson, N. J.: St. Anthony Guild Press).
20. Mary Aurelia, Sister, with F. M. Kirsch, *Practical Aids for Catholic Teachers*, Vol. I & II (Chicago: Benziger).
21. Milady, Thomas, *Saints for Home and School* (Milwaukee: Bruce).
22. Montani, *St. Gregory Hymnal* (Philadelphia: St. Gregory Guild, Inc.).
23. *New Saint Basil Hymnal*, Willis Music Co., 124 Fourth St., Cincinnati.
24. O'Connor, J. F., S.J., *Chalk Talks*, Parts I, II, III, IV (St. Louis: The Queen's Work).
25. Schumaker, Rt. Rev. Msgr. M., *I Teach Catechism*, Vols. I & II (New York: Benziger).
26. Tonne, Arthur, O.F.M., *Series of Talks for Children* (Emporia, Kans.: Didde Printing Co.).
27. World Library of Sacred Music, *People's Hymnal*, 1846 Westwood Avenue, Cincinnati 14, Ohio.

AUDIO-VISUAL MATERIALS

A. Motion Pictures
1. Catechetical Guild Educational Society, 147 East 5th St., St. Paul 1, Minn.
   The Mass
2. Catholic Movie Distributors, 220 West 42nd St., New York, N. Y.
   Passion Play

B. Slides
1. Catechetical Guild
   Mass Slides
2. Society for Visual Education, 100 E. Ohio St., Chicago, Ill.
   Life of Christ

C. Filmstrips
1. Society for Visual Education
   First Communion Series
   Bible Books for Small People Series
   Hail Mary — Rosary — Records
2. St. John's University, Brooklyn, N. Y.
   The Creed (Series of 10 filmstrips and recordings)
   The Sacraments (Filmstrips and recordings)
3. Catechetical Guild
   The Mass for Young Children
   The Life of Our Lord, as told by His Mother
   God's Story Book
   The Rosary
   My Confession

D. Recordings
1. Catechetical Guild
   Catholic Children's Record Library — 12 records of the Life of Christ
   Educational Sales Dept.
2. Catholic Educational Recordings, Educational Sales Dept., RCA Victor Division, Camden, N. J.
   Series A and B Lives of the Saints
   Stories from the Faith and Freedom Readers

E. Pictures
1. Catechetical Guild
   Ten Commandments
   Apostles' Creed
   Seven Sacraments
   Mysteries of the Rosary
   I Live the Rosary
   Eighty Mass Photos
   Life of Christ
   Window Transparencies
2. Sister M. Edmunda, B.V.M., 4637 N. Ashland, Chicago 40, Ill.
   Feast Days of Our Lady (12 pictures)
   Bible Stories (12 pictures)
3. Apostolate of the Press, Society of St. Paul, 2187 Victory Blvd., Staten Island 14, N. Y.
   Jan's Day
   The Children's Seven Spiritual Works of Mercy
   The Children's Seven Corporal Works of Mercy
4. Co-op Parish Activities Service, Effingham, Ill.
   Life of Christ

F. Charts
1. Catechetical Guild
   Prayer Charts

G. Coloring Books
1. Father Francis, 1501 S. Layton Blvd., Milwaukee 15, Wis.
   The King Comes
   Our Mother Mary
   The Childhood of Jesus
   Jesus Is God
   Stories Jesus Told
   I Follow Jesus
   The Catholic Child
   The Holy Rosary
   They Became Saints
   Around the Year in Picture and Song
   The Catholic Child Goes to Mass
2. Catechetical Guild
   Talking to God
   The Story of Our Lady
   Meet Your Angel
   It's a Joy to Go to Church
   Meet the Family
   The Rose Queen
   I Believe in God
   The Saints Are My Friends
   God Is Wonderful
   How Jesus Lived
   A World of Friends
   The First Story

H. Miscellaneous
1. Catechetical Guild
   Mass flannel board and figures

UNIT ONE. WE BELONG TO GOD

(Text, *God's Truths Help Us Live*, pp. 11–44)

(Revised Baltimore Catechism No. 1 [Confraternity] Questions 1 to 7.)

INTRODUCTORY MATERIALS

I. INTRODUCTION FOR THE TEACHER

In this unit, the child will be brought to an understanding of the purpose of his existence and to a knowledge of how God's truths have been made known to us, namely: through Creation and Revelation. In the presentation of this unit, instructions and discussions on Creation will be brief, since a great part of Unit Three is devoted to that subject.

A review of the sacraments of penance and Holy Eucharist, so necessary at the beginning of the third grade, is placed in logical sequence in the outline, but should be used earlier than the time specified if the teacher sees the need for doing so.

II. OBJECTIVES OF THE UNIT

A. To arouse in the children a great desire to know God better in order to love and serve Him faithfully.
B. To lead the children to the practice of the virtue of faith.
C. To review the sacraments of penance and Holy Eucharist.

III. SUBJECT MATTER

A. Who made us?
B. Who God is
C. Why God made us
D. What we must do to gain the happiness of heaven
E. How we learn to know, love, and serve God
   1. By Creation
   2. Through Revelation
   3. Through the Catholic Church
F. Where we can find the chief truths taught by Jesus Christ through the Catholic Church
G. A review of the prayer, the Apostles' Creed

IV. TEACHER REFERENCES FOR UNIT ONE

1. Baierl, *The Creed Explained*, pp. 17–75.
2. Belger, *Sing a Song of Holy Things*, pp. 1, 2, 12, 15, 86, 87, 92, 93, 97.
3. Brennan, *Angel Food*, pp. 35–37.
4. Brennan, *Going His Way*, pp. 63–66.
5. Johnson, *The Bible Story*, pp. 79–81, 94–98.
6. Kelly, *Balt. Cat. No. 1 With Dev.*, pp. 2–11; 105–157.
7. Lovasik, *Catechism Sketched*, pp. 1–6, 72–79, 89–121.
8. Montani, *St. Gregory Hymnal*, pp. 39, 53.
9. Noll, *Religion and Life*, Vol. I, pp. 85–96.
10. *People's Hymnal*, T-10.
11. Thayer, *The Child on His Knees*, pp. 60, 64, 65.
12. Schumacher, *I Teach Catechism*, Vol. I, p. 114.
13. *New Saint Basil's Hymnal*, Willis Music Co., Cincinnati, Ohio.

LESSON PLANS FOR UNIT ONE

I. Introduction to Unit One

We Belong to God. Text, p. 11

LESSON PLAN 1

I. SUBJECT MATTER
We Belong to God

II. TYPE
Introduction

III. OBJECTIVES
A. To prepare the children for a new unit of work.
B. To instill in the children a desire to learn.
C. To stimulate the children to do good thinking.

IV. MATERIALS
Unit I, p. 11 sqq., in the children's texts.

V. PROCEDURE

A. Approach
Today we are going to try to remember some of the things we learned about God in the second grade. On page 10 in your text you will find a "Memory Box."

B. Presentation
1. "Memory Box"
   a) The children read each question and try to answer it.
   b) A discussion of the answers will follow.

c) Proceed in this way with all the questions in the "Memory Box."

d) The children ask questions they want answered in this unit. (The teacher writes the questions on the board as they are given.) The children discuss the sources of information available for the material of this unit. The children suggest any activities they would like to carry out in this unit (e.g., learn some songs or poems about God and heaven).

2. Summary:

The children summarize the things they intend to learn about in this unit.

The children discuss why they want to learn these truths (e.g., to understand better the things they must know in order to love and serve God perfectly).

II. Work Study Periods for Unit One
(Lesson Plans 2–21)

UNIT ONE, PART 1, God Made Us to Share in His Happiness. Text, p. 12

LESSON PLAN 2

> "The Father Himself loves you . . ." (Jn. 16:27).
> Blackboard

I. SUBJECT MATTER
Who God Is and Why He Made Us

II. TYPE
Development

III. OBJECTIVES
A. To develop the idea that God is the Supreme Being.
B. To develop the knowledge that God made us to share His happiness.
C. To help the children acquire a great love for God because He made us.
D. To incite in the children acts of gratitude toward God for His goodness to them.

IV. MATERIALS
Story — "The Little Girl Who Didn't Want to Go to Heaven," Brennan, *Going His Way*, pp. 63–66.

V. PROCEDURE
A. Approach
Ask questions — Who made us? Who is God?

B. Presentation
1. Explanation and discussion:
    a) Recall the children's former concept of God:
    1) A spirit who cannot be seen with our eyes.
    2) Our heavenly Father
    b) Explain that God made us. That God is the Supreme Being; define the term; explain why God is the Supreme Being.
    c) Explain and discuss God's purpose for making us:
    1) To show His goodness. He didn't have to make us, but did so because He is good and wanted to show His goodness to us.
    2) To share with us His everlasting happiness in heaven.
        (*a*) Explain that God was always very happy in heaven. He didn't need anything or anyone to make Him happy, but wanted to share His happiness with us, so He made us.
        (*b*) Explain that some day we will share God's happiness in heaven if we are good while here on earth.
        (*c*) Discuss: How long will heaven last? What will heaven be like?
        (*d*) Compare God's goodness to us with the goodness of our parents.
        (*e*) End the presentation by repeating the exact answers of the Revised Baltimore Catechism No. 1 (Confraternity), questions 1–3.

2. Application:
Do you think that God loves us very much? How can you tell? How can we show God that we appreciate His goodness to us?

3. Organization:
    a) Who is God?
    b) Why is God called the Supreme Being?
    c) Why did God make us?
    d) Why is God willing to share His happiness with us?

4. Broader Appreciation:
Story — "The Little Girl Who Didn't Want to Go to Heaven," Brennan, *Going His Way*, pp. 63–66.

5. Assignment:
Catechism questions 1, 2, 3, at the end of Unit I in children's texts, *God's Truths Help Us Live*, p. 39.*

UNIT ONE, PART 1, (cont.). Text, p. 13

LESSON PLAN 3

> "My God, I Love Thee" (Raccolta, 39).
> Blackboard

---

* Here, as in each succeeding lesson, these Catechism questions and answers will be found in the pupil's text, *God's Truths Help Us Live*.

I. SUBJECT MATTER

What We Must Do to Share God's Happiness. (Know, Love, Serve)

II. TYPE

Development

III. OBJECTIVES

A. To develop the knowledge of what we must do to share God's happiness.
B. To instill in the children greater desire to know, love, and serve God.
C. To lead the children to better their actions as a preparation for heaven.

IV. MATERIALS

Poem: "God and I," Sister Josita Belger, *Sing a Song of Holy Things*, p. 1.

V. PROCEDURE

A. Approach

If you made a toy out of wood, could you say the toy belonged to you? If so, why? (Because I made it.) Could you use it the way you want? Could you tell other children who use it how you want the toy handled?

B. Presentation

1. Explanation and discussion:
   a) Explain that since God made all things, all things belong to Him; He may use these things as He pleases; He is the one to say how these things should be used; He is the one to say what the things He made are to do.
   b) Explain that since God made us to live in heaven with Him some day, He expects us to do certain things to get there. Explain and discuss the three things that He wants us to do to get to heaven.
      1) Know God.
         (a) Discuss: Did you ever see the President of the United States? Do you know him? How do you know about him?
         (b) Discuss: Do you know God? Did you ever see Him? How do you know about Him?
         (c) Explain that God helps us know Him in two big ways; explain that tomorrow's lesson will be about the two big ways in which we learn to know God.
      2) Love God.
         (a) Compare the love we have for our parents with the love we have for strangers. Discuss: Why do we love our parents more than we love strangers? Explain that the more we learn to know our parents and the more we learn to know about their goodness to us, the more we love them.
         (b) Explain that the more we learn about God and His goodness to us, the more we will love Him. Explain that all our lives we must try to know God better so we will love Him more.
         (c) Discuss the degree of love that God expects from us.
      3) Serve God.
         (a) Explain that to serve God means to do as He wants us to do.
         (b) Discuss: How do we know what God wants us to do?
         (c) Discuss: How do we serve our parents? Why? Why do some children obey and help their parents more than other children do? Explain that those who serve God the best love Him the most. Give examples of ways in which great love for God is expressed in loving service.
         (d) Give a chalk talk to illustrate how we get to heaven by knowing, loving, serving God.
         (e) End the presentation by repeating exact answer of the Revised Baltimore Catechism No. 1 (Confraternity) question 4, Text, p. 39.

2. Application:

Hasn't God made it easy for us to get to heaven? The children resolve to do their best to know, love, and serve God now, so that some day they may gain the happiness of heaven.

3. Organization:
   a) What three things must we do to get to heaven some day?
   b) Why must we know God before we can love Him?
   c) How do we serve God?
   d) What kind of children serve God the best?

4. Broader Appreciation:

Poem — "God and I," Sister Josita Belger, *Sing a Song of Holy Things*, p. 1.

5. Assignment:

Catechism question 4, p. 39, at the end of Unit I in children's texts.

6. Suggested Activity:

The children practice writing:
   To get to heaven I must know, love, and serve God.

UNIT ONE, PART 1 (cont.). Text, p. 14

LESSON PLAN 4

"My God and my all" (Raccolta, 5).

Blackboard

11

I. **SUBJECT MATTER**
How We Learn To Know God

II. **TYPE**
Development

III. **OBJECTIVES**
A. To lead the children to an understanding of how we learn to know God.
B. To lead the children to an appreciation of the help that God gives them to know Him.
C. To lead the children to use God's helps in knowing Him.

IV. **MATERIALS**
A. A large picture of a beautiful dog.
B. Poem: "Messages," Thayer, *The Child on His Knees*, 64–65.

V. **PROCEDURE**

A. Approach
Recall the three things that we must do to get to heaven. (Know, love, and serve God.) Recall the fact that we can't love and serve God unless we first *know* Him. Explain that today we are going to learn about two ways in which God has made Himself known to the world so that all may love and serve Him.

B. Presentation
1. Explanation and discussion:
   a) Show the children a picture of a beautiful dog. The children study the picture and discuss the artist who drew it. (He must be a gifted person; he must love animals, etc.)
   b) Explain that although God does not show Himself to us today, we can learn many things about Him just by looking at the things He made. Give examples to show how Creation teaches us to know God:
   1) All things here on earth had a beginning.
   2) The sun tells us of God's great power.
   3) The good food that God puts here on the earth for us shows that He is a loving Father who takes care of His children.
   4) The very fact that God made me and lets me live shows that He loves me very much.
      (a) The children give examples to show how Creation teaches them about God.
   c) Explain that God has made Himself known to us in another way too. Explain that long before Jesus came upon the earth to live, God often spoke to His friends here on the earth because He wanted them to know, love, and serve Him.
   1) He told these friends some things about Himself (e.g., "I am the Lord Thy God").
   2) He told these friends some things that He wanted them to do (e.g., God told Moses to lead God's people from a faraway land to one that He had chosen for them). Explain that this year we will hear and read about the things that God said to some of His friends so that we will see how He made many of His truths known to the world.
   3) Children discuss people to whom God spoke long ago — Adam, Moses, etc.

2. Application:
   How wonderful God is to make Himself known to us. If we had no way of knowing that there is a God in heaven, how could we ever hope to love Him and serve Him here on this earth? The children resolve to learn as much as they can about their Father in heaven by looking at and thinking about the things God made, and by learning the truths God has made known to us.

3. Organization:
   The children think of some of the things that God made and the truths that these things teach them about God.

4. Broader Appreciation:
   Poem — "Message," Thayer, *The Child on His Knees*, pp. 64–65.

5. Assignment:
   None

6. Suggested Activity:
   The children find pictures of some things that God made.

UNIT ONE, PART 1, (cont.).

LESSON PLAN 5

The children read or reread and discuss Part I, Text, pp. 12–15.

UNIT ONE, PART 2, LESSON PLANS 6–8, God Teaches Us How to Gain Heaven. Text, pp. 16–19

LESSON PLAN 6

> "God has visited His people" (Lk. 7:16).
> Blackboard

I. **SUBJECT MATTER**
God teaches us how to gain heaven. (Through Church)

II. **TYPE**
Development

III. **OBJECTIVES**
A. To develop the understanding of how the Cath-

olic Church teaches us to know, love, and serve God.
- B. To lead the children to an appreciation of the teachings of the Catholic Church.
- C. To instill in the children the practice of faith.

IV. MATERIALS
None

V. PROCEDURE

A. Approach
Recall the two ways in which God has made Himself known to the world — through the things He made and the things He said.

B. Presentation
1. Explanation and discussion:
   - *a)* Explain that the best way in which we can know about God and His truths is by learning about the things that God has told us through the words of His Son. Give examples of some of God's truths that Jesus has revealed.
     1) God is our loving Father who takes care of us.
     2) Heaven is for all those who do the will of God.
     3) God takes care of the things He made; God will take care of us.
   - *b)* Discuss: Since Jesus is not preaching and teaching on this earth today, how can we learn God's truths from Him? Explain that when Jesus was on the earth, He founded the Catholic Church; He taught the Apostles all the things that they must teach others about God and the things God wants us to do to live with Him some day. Explain that the Catholic Church continued after the Apostles.
   - *c)* Explain that the twelve most important truths that Jesus taught the Apostles were written into a prayer that we already know — the Apostles' Creed. Explain that we are going to study each of these truths this year so that we will know more about God and His truths, so we can love Him more, and serve Him better.
   - *d)* End the presentation by repeating exact answers of the Revised Baltimore Catechism No. 1 (Confraternity), questions 5, 6, 7, Text, pp. 39, 40.
   - *e)* Review the prayer: The Apostles' Creed.
2. Application:
   What is the best way in which we can learn to know God today? (By learning the truths that the Catholic Church teaches.) The children resolve to listen to and believe all that the Catholic Church teaches because the Church teaches the word of God. The children resolve to listen attentively to the priest when he reads the word of God.
3. Organization:
   List with the children the persons and things that will help them learn what the Catholic Church teaches:
   - *a)* Priests
   - *b)* Sisters
   - *c)* Parents
   - *d)* Religious books at school or home
   - *e)* Religion texts (Catholic only)
4. Broader Appreciation:
   The children devoutly recite the "Apostles' Creed."
5. Assignment:
   Catechism questions 5, 6, and 7, pp. 39, 40, at the end of Unit I in children's texts.
6. Suggested Activity:
   Have the children write the Apostles' Creed.

UNIT ONE, PART 2, (cont.). Text, p. 16

LESSON PLAN 7

The children read or reread and discuss Part II, pp. 16–20, in their texts.

UNIT ONE, PART 2, (cont.). Text, p. 17

LESSON PLAN 8

I. SUBJECT MATTER
Knowing, Loving, and Serving God

II. TYPE
Discussion

III. OBJECTIVES
- A. To lead the children to a better understanding and appreciation of the subject studied.
- B. To lead the children to apply the truths learned in Parts I–II of the unit to daily living.

IV. MATERIALS
Children's text, Unit I, Parts I and II, pp. 12–16.

V. PROCEDURE

A. Approach
Let's see if we know why God put us on this earth.

B. Presentation
1. Set up standards for the discussion.
   - *a)* The children formulate a few rules to be followed while carrying on the discussion.
     1) Keep to the subject
     2) Everyone take part
     3) Speak distinctly
     4) Help others take part
     5) Be courteous
     6) Be good listeners

b) The teacher writes these rules on the board.
2. Present for the discussion the material found in the children's texts under "Things to Talk About," and "Problems."
3. Generalization:
   a) The children give some important points in the form of statements which they wish to remember as a conclusion of this discussion.
   b) End presentation by repeating exact answers of the Baltimore Catechism No. 1 (Confraternity), questions 1–7, Text, pp. 39–40.
4. Application:
   The children formulate resolutions resulting from the discussion.
5. Assignment:
   Review Catechism questions 1–7, pp. 39–40 in Text.
6. Suggested Activity:
   Children write their resolutions and check each day to see whether they are keeping them.

UNIT ONE, PARTS 3 AND 4, LESSONS 9 AND 10, Jesus Helps Us Know, Love, and Serve God. Text, pp. 20–21

Penance — A Cure for Sick Souls. Text, pp. 20–22

LESSON PLAN 9

> "My Jesus, mercy" (Raccolta, 70).
> Blackboard

I. SUBJECT MATTER
Jesus Helps Us Know, Love, and Serve God. (Sacrament of Penance)

II. TYPE
Development

III. OBJECTIVES
A. To develop in the children the knowledge of the help (grace) that Jesus gives us in knowing, loving, and serving God.
B. To help develop a better understanding of the sacrament of Penance.
C. To develop a greater appreciation of God's love in giving us help in knowing, loving, and serving him.
D. To lead the children to receive the sacrament of Penance often.

IV. MATERIALS
Poem: "Sin," Sister Josita Belger, *Sing a Song of Holy Things,* p. 86.
Picture: Easter Sunday Evening: Jesus Appearing to the Apostles.

V. PROCEDURE

A. Approach
Discuss: How can we best find out how to know, love, and serve God? (From Jesus who teaches us through the Catholic Church.) Do you think we need any help in learning to know, love, and serve God?

B. Presentation
1. Explanation and discussion:
   a) Explain that Jesus loves us so much that He helps us to know, love, and serve His Father in heaven. Discuss very briefly what grace is and what it does. (Do not go into detail at this time.)
   b) Discuss briefly the ways in which we get grace: through prayer and the sacraments.
   c) Explain that Penance is one great sacrament that helps us know, love, and serve God.
      1) Discuss what the sacrament of Penance is.
      2) Discuss the institution (show picture) and purpose of this sacrament.
      3) Explain and discuss how the priest gets the power to forgive sins.
      4) Explain and discuss what the sacrament of Penance does and how it shows God's goodness to us.
         (a) Takes away sin committed after baptism.
         (b) Gives us grace to be good.
         (c) Makes our souls holy and pleasing to God.
      5) Discuss the necessity for frequent confession.
2. Application:
   Thank God for giving us the sacrament of penance. How can you do this? How often shall we try to receive this sacrament?
3. Organization:
   a) Who helps us to know, love, and serve God better? How?
   b) How does the sacrament of Penance help us know God better?
   c) How will the sacrament of Penance help us serve God better?
   d) When did Jesus give us the sacrament of Penance?
   e) What must we do if we want our sins forgiven?
   f) What three things does the sacrament of Penance do for us?
4. Broader Appreciation:
   Poem — "Sin," Sister Josita Belger, *Sing a Song of Holy Things,* p. 86.
5. Assignment:
   None
6. Suggested Activity:
   The children make up a short prayer to thank God for giving us the sacrament of Penance.
   The children draw pictures to illustrate a priest using his power to forgive sin.

UNIT ONE, PARTS 3, 4 (cont.). Text, pp. 20–22

LESSON PLAN 10

The children read or reread and discuss Parts 3 and 4, pp. 20–22 in their texts.

UNIT ONE, PART 5, LESSONS 11–13, How to Receive the Sacrament of Penance Worthily. Text, pp. 25–28

LESSON PLANS 11–12
(Two-Day Plan)

> "O God, be merciful to me, the sinner" (Lk. 18:13).
> Blackboard

I. SUBJECT MATTER
What Is Necessary to Receive the Sacrament of Penance Worthily.

II. TYPE
Development

III. OBJECTIVES
A. To broaden the children's understanding of how to receive the sacrament of Penance worthily.
B. To help the children show appreciation toward God for His mercy.
C. To reteach the formula for confession.
D. To instill a sincere desire to receive the sacrament of Penance well.

IV. MATERIALS
Poem — "Pardon Me, Jesus," Sister Josita Belger, *Sing a Song of Holy Things*, p. 87.
Story — "The Most Beautiful Thing in the World," Brennan, *Angel Food*, pp. 35–37.

V. PROCEDURE

A. Approach
Do you remember what the sacrament of Penance is? What does it do for you? Today we will learn what is necessary to receive the sacrament of Penance well.

B. Presentation
1. Explanation and discussion:
    a) Explain that to make a good confession we need the help of the Holy Ghost; He is the one who will open up our minds so that we will know our sins; He is the one who will help us be truly sorry; He is the one who will help us tell our sins truthfully.
        1) Discuss short prayers or ejaculations we can say to the Holy Ghost before confession.
    b) Reteach and discuss thoroughly the five things necessary to recive the sacrament of Penance worthily:
        1) I must think of my sins.
            (a) Define the phrase: examine our conscience; discuss briefly how our conscience works.
            (b) Go over the Ten Commandments, formulating and discussing the sins against each. (This will take at least one religion lesson.)
        2) I must be sorry for my sins.
            (a) Discuss the kind of sorrow for sin we must have.
            (b) Discuss the sorrow of Judas and St. Peter.
            (c) Explain that sorrow for sin is the most important part of going to confession; explain why.
        3) I must make up my mind not to sin again.
            (a) Discuss why this part of confession preparation is necessary; explain that this will be the true test of our sorrow.
            (b) Explain that we must stay away from the people, places, and things that lead us into sin.
        4) I must tell my sins to the priest.
            (a) Reteach the formula for confession.
            (b) Discuss the necessity for being sincere and truthful in going to confession.
            (c) Discuss the necessity for politeness to the priest.
            (d) Explain and discuss why we must never be afraid when we go to confession.
        5) I must say the penance that the priest gives me.
            (a) Explain and discuss the kind of penance we receive, the reason for receiving and saying this penance.
            (b) Explain the necessity for saying this penance immediately after confession.
            (c) Discuss other little penances we can do to make up for our sins and the sins of others.

2. Application:
The children resolve to prepare well for each confession and to receive the sacrament of penance as well and as often as they can.

3. Organization:
List on the board with the children the five things necessary to receive the sacrament of Penance worthily.

4. Broader Appreciation:
Poem — "Pardon Me, Jesus," Sister Josita Belger, *Sing a Sing of Holy Things*, p. 87.
Story — "The Most Beautiful Thing in the World," Brennan, *Angel Food*, pp. 35–37.

5. Assignment:
None.

6. Suggested Activity:
   The children trace their hand on paper and write the five things necessary for confession in the five fingers.
   The children plan and make a frieze to show themselves preparing for and receiving the sacrament of Penance.

UNIT ONE, PART 5, How to Receive the Sacrament of Penance Worthily. Text, pp. 25–28

LESSON PLAN 13

I. SUBJECT MATTER
The Sacrament of Penance

II. TYPE
Discussion

III. MATERIALS
Children's Text, Unit I, Parts 3, 4, 5, pp. 20–28.

IV. PROCEDURE
Same as for discussion plan found in Unit I — Lesson 8.

UNIT ONE, PART 5 (cont.).

LESSON PLAN 14

The children read or reread and discuss Part 5, p. 25, in their text.

UNIT ONE, PARTS 6 AND 7, The Holy Eucharist. Text, pp. 29–31
Holy Communion — Food for Our Souls. Text, pp. 31–33

LESSON PLAN 15

> "O Sacrament most holy, O Sacrament divine! All praise and all thanksgiving be every moment Thine!" (Raccolta, 136).
> **Blackboard**

I. SUBJECT MATTER
The Sacrament of Holy Eucharist

II. TYPE
Development

III. OBJECTIVES
A. To bring the children to a greater knowledge and love of God because of His love in giving us the sacrament of Holy Eucharist.
B. To instill in the hearts and minds of the children a greater love and appreciation for Jesus in the Blessed Sacrament.
C. To arouse in the children the desire to receive and visit Jesus often.

IV. MATERIALS
A. A large picture of the Last Supper.
B. Poem — "The Answer," Thayer, *The Child on His Knees*, p. 60.

V. PROCEDURE

A. Approach
Today we are going to talk about one of the greatest ways in which we can receive grace to know, love, and serve God better.

B. Presentation
1. Explanation and discussion:
   a) Discuss informally the children's previous knowledge of the sacrament of Holy Eucharist; discuss the names for this sacrament — Blessed Sacrament, Holy Communion — and the times when each term is used.
   b) Show a picture of the Last Supper; recall the institution of the Holy Eucharist.
   c) Recall that the Apostles were given the power to change bread and wine into the Body and Blood of Jesus at the Last Supper; discuss how the priest receives this same power and uses it at every Mass.
   d) Explain and discuss:
      1) Why Jesus remains with us in the Tabernacle.
         (a) He wants to be near us so we can come to visit Him.
         (b) He wants to be our daily food.
      2) Why Jesus gives Himself to us in Holy Communion.
         (a) To prove His great love for us.
         (b) To give us grace to be good.
         (c) To make us more holy and pleasing to God.
         (d) To help us know, love, and serve Him better.
         (e) Discuss the following:
            (1) Our Lord's great goodness in giving us Himself in the Holy Eucharist.
            (2) How often the children should try to visit Jesus in the Blessed Sacrament.
            (3) How often the children should try to receive Holy Communion.
2. Applications:
   The children resolve to return God's goodness to them by receiving and visiting Jesus as often as they can.
3. Organization:
   a) When did Jesus first give us the sacrament

of the Holy Eucharist?
- b) Why did Jesus change bread and wine into His Body and Blood?
- c) When does the priest change bread and wine into the Body and Blood of Jesus?
- d) Where did the priest get such a wonderful power?
- e) How often should we try to visit Jesus in the Blessed Sacrament? Why?
- f) How often should we try to receive Holy Communion? Why?

4. Broader Appreciation:
   Poem — "The Answer."

5. Assignment:
   None

6. Suggested Activity:
   The children practice writing the prayer, "O Sacrament most holy . . ." etc., and memorize it.

UNIT ONE, PARTS 6 AND 7 (cont.).

LESSON PLAN 16

The children read or reread and discuss Unit I, Parts 6 and 7, pp. 29–31, in their texts.

UNIT ONE, PART 8, LESSON PLANS 17–21, What I Must Do Each Time I Receive Jesus. Text, pp. 34–36

LESSON PLAN 17

> "Behold, thy king comes to thee" (Mt. 21:5).
> Blackboard

I. SUBJECT MATTER
What I Must Do Each Time I Receive Jesus

II. TYPE
Development

III. OBJECTIVES
A. To instruct the children in the proper preparation for Holy Communion.
B. To arouse in the children the desire to prepare fervently for each Holy Communion.
C. To instill in the children a great love for Jesus in the Blessed Sacrament.

IV. MATERIALS
Poem — "A Throne for My King," Sister Josita Belger, *Sing a Song of Holy Things*, pp. 92–93.

V. PROCEDURE
A. Approach
Discuss ways in which we prepare for the coming of a great visitor to our home. Explain that today we are going to talk about getting ready for the greatest visitor that will ever come to us — the King of the world.

B. Presentation
1. Explanation and discussion:
   a) Explain thoroughly the preparation children must make for each Holy Communion.
      1) I must be free from mortal sin.
         (a) Explain what we must do to have mortal sin taken from us.
         (b) Explain why we must be free from mortal sin each time we receive Holy Communion.
         (c) Explain what we should do before we receive Holy Communion if we are guilty of venial sin.
         (d) Explain why we do not have to go to confession each time we wish to receive Holy Communion if we are guilty of venial sin only. (However, recommend frequent confession.)
      2) I must be fasting.
         (a) Explain what this fast is and when this fast begins; explain new rules on fasting.
         (b) Explain why we should not receive Holy Communion when we are not fasting.
      3) I must pray (discuss the kinds of prayers we should say before we receive Holy Communion):
         (a) Prayers in our own words. (The children give examples.)
         (b) Prayers before Holy Communion found in our prayer books.
   b) Discuss again the necessity for frequent Holy Communion; explain how to make a spiritual communion if we are unable to receive sacramentally when we go to Mass.

2. Application:
   The children resolve to prepare well for each Holy Communion at each Mass they attend.

3. Organization:
   List on the board with the children the things they must do each time they wish to receive Holy Communion.

4. Broader Appreciation:
   Poem — "A Throne for My King," Sister Josita Belger, *Sing a Song of Holy Things*, pp. 92–93.

5. Assignment:
   None

6. Suggested Activities:
   The children draw a picture of themselves preparing for Holy Communion.
   The children write short prayers and place them around the picture that they have made.

UNIT ONE, PART 8 (cont.). Text, pp. 35–36

LESSON PLAN 18

> "My Lord and my God" (Raccolta, 133).
> Blackboard

I. **SUBJECT MATTER**
Receiving and Thanking Jesus

II. **TYPE**
Development

III. **OBJECTIVES**
A. To teach proper practices for and thanksgiving after Holy Communion.
B. To instill in the hearts of the children gratitude to God.
C. To create in the children a desire to thank God fervently after each Holy Communion.

IV. **MATERIALS**
Poem — "After Holy Communion," Sister Josita Belger, *Sing a Song of Holy Things*, p. 97.

V. **PROCEDURE**

A. Approach
Review with children what they must do each time they prepare for Holy Communion — be free from mortal sin, be fasting, pray.

B. Presentation
1. Explanation and discussion:
    a) Discuss the proper way the children should go to the communion rail to receive Holy Communion; practice walking, folding hands, kneeling quietly and correctly.
    b) Explain and discuss what the children should do while they are waiting at the communion rail — be devout, close eyes, put out tongue, remain at the rail until person next to you has received, go back to seat properly and reverently.
    c) Explain and discuss what the children should do after they return to their seats:
    1) Talk to Jesus in their own words.
        (a) Discuss what the children should talk about; help them formulate prayers to say.
        (b) Discuss what the children should do with their eyes while they are talking to Jesus.
    2) Say the prayers after Holy Communion in their prayer books.
    d) Call attention to the Prayer Before a Crucifix in their prayer books; explain why the children should read it after Holy Communion. (Explain the words of the prayer briefly.)

2. Application
The children resolve to use the time after Holy Communion well and to make their whole day a thank-you prayer.
3. Organization:
List on the board with the children the things they should do before and after each Holy Communion.
4. Broader Appreciation:
Poem — "After Holy Communion," Sister Josita Belger, *Sing a Song of Holy Things*, p. 97.
5. Suggested Activities:
The children draw a picture of themselves after Holy Communion.
The children write short prayers they have made up and place them around the picture.

UNIT ONE, PART 8 (cont.).

LESSON PLAN 19

The children read or reread and discuss Part 8, p. 34, in their texts.

UNIT ONE, PART 8 (cont.).

LESSON PLAN 20

I. **SUBJECT MATTER**
The Holy Eucharist

II. **TYPE**
Discussion

III. **MATERIALS**
Children's text, "Problems" at the end of Unit I, p. 37.

IV. **PROCEDURE**
Same as for discussion plan found in Unit I — Lesson 8 in the Manual.

UNIT ONE, PART 8 (cont.).

LESSON PLAN 21

I. **SUBJECT MATTER**
We Belong to God

II. **TYPE**
Drill on Unit

III. **OBJECTIVES**
A. To check orally on the children's mastery of the material taken in this unit.
B. To apply knowledge obtained in this unit to daily living.

IV. MATERIALS
Questions at the end of Unit I, p. 40.

V. PROCEDURE

A. Approach
Today we are going to see how much we have learned during our study of Unit One.
Do you think you will know all the answers?

B. Presentation
1. The children answer orally all the questions.
2. Clear up mistaken ideas developed in the minds of any individuals during the study of this unit.
3. Application:
    Do you think you have learned many truths about God and His goodness to us in this unit? Is it important to do what is right because of what we have learned? The children resolve to be better children because of the things they learned in this unit.
4. Assignment:
    Review Catechism questions 1–7, Text, pp. 39–40, at the end of Unit I.

III. Culmination of Unit One

LESSON PLAN 22

I. SUBJECT MATTER
We Belong to God

II. TYPE
Culmination

III. OBJECTIVES
  A. To summarize the concepts learned in this unit.
  B. To apply the knowledge obtained in this unit to daily living.
  C. To plan and give a little program as a culmination of the unit.

IV. MATERIALS
Hymns, poems, stories, etc., developed during this unit.

V. PROCEDURE

A. Approach
Today we are going to try to remember the truths that we have learned during this unit. Have you learned very many of God's truths? How well do you remember them?

B. Generalization
The children use their books to find and give in the form of statements the truths they want to remember because of their study of this unit. (Cf. Things to Remember.)

C. Application:
The children think of and tell some of the things that they want to do from now on so they can apply the truths learned in this unit to everyday living. The teacher may list them on the blackboard as they are given.

D. Planning:
The children think of some of the activities they have carried on during the presentation of this unit. They plan a little program using these various activities.

E. Practice of program to be used as culminating activity.
This can be done during "extra minutes" of the school day.

F. Classroom program (culminating activity):
This can be given in the next religion or English period.

IV. Evaluation of Unit One

LESSON PLAN 23

The children take the written test found at the end of Unit One, pp. 41–44 in their texts.
After each Unit, reteach and retest where there are weaknesses revealed.

SPECIAL LESSON PLANS FOR THE LITURGICAL YEAR (Unit One)

*September 8 — Nativity of Mary
   Prayer: "Holy Mother of God, pray for us." (*Raccolta*, 319)
September 12 — Holy Name of Mary
   Prayer: "Mary." (*Raccolta*, 292)
September 15 — The Seven Sorrows of Mary
   Prayer: "Mother of love, of sorrow, and of mercy, pray for us." (*Raccolta*, 300)
*September 29 — St. Michael the Archangel
   Prayer: "St. Michael, pray for us." (*Raccolta*, 687)
October 2 — Guardian Angels
   Prayer: "All ye holy angels and archangels, pray for us." (*Raccolta*, 687)
October 3 — St. Therese of the Child Jesus
   Prayer: "O Saint Therese of the Child Jesus, Patroness of the Missions, pray for us." (*Raccolta*, 574)
October 4 — St. Francis of Assisi
   Prayer: "St. Francis, pray for us." (*Raccolta*, 687)
*October 7 — The Holy Rosary
   Prayer: "Queen of the most holy Rosary, pray for us." (*Raccolta*, 319)
   * *Feasts to be developed thoroughly; lesson plans for each follow.*

LESSON PLAN FOR THE NATIVITY OF THE BLESSED VIRGIN MARY

I. SUBJECT MATTER

Feast of the Nativity of Mary

II. TYPE

Development

III. OBJECTIVES

A. To give an understanding of the purpose of this feast.
B. To teach a new prayer to say after Sunday Mass.
C. To increase love for Mary.

IV. MATERIALS

Prayer — "Hail, Holy Queen," Text, p 7.
Poem — "Mary's Birthday," Sister Josita Belger, *Sing a Song of Holy Things*, p. 2.

V. PROCEDURE

A. Approach

Does anyone know whose feast this is?

B. Presentation

1. Explanation and discussion:
   a) Explain the purpose of today's feast.
   b) Select at least one virtue to practice today.
   c) Explain the words of, and teach, the new prayer, "Hail, Holy Queen."
2. Application:
   The children resolve to pray often to Mary.
3. Organization:
   The children compose an original prayer to Mary, dedicating the school year to her.
4. Broader Appreciation:
   Poem — "Mary's Birthday."
5. Suggested Activity:
   The children practice writing either the prayer, "Hail, Holy Queen," or the original prayer just composed.

LESSON PLAN FOR THE FEAST OF ST. MICHAEL

I. SUBJECT MATTER

Feast of St. Michael

II. TYPE

Development

III. OBJECTIVES

A. To give an understanding of today's feast.
B. To teach a new prayer.
C. To encourage dependence upon the help of St. Michael when it is needed.

IV. MATERIALS

Prayer — "St. Michael the Archangel," Text, p. 7.
A large picture of the fall of the bad angels.

V. PROCEDURE

A. Approach

Show the large picture to the children.
Discuss. What is it about? Why was it put up in the classroom today?

B. Presentation

1. Explanation and discussion:
   a) Recall the story of St. Michael as learned in previous years.
   b) Discuss St. Michael's great power over the devil, even today; discuss the times when we need St. Michael to help us.
   c) Teach the prayer, "St. Michael, the Archangel," after explaining the words.
2. Application:
   Do you think St. Michael was very brave? Why? The children resolve to ask St. Michael for his help to do what is right when the devil and his helpers try to make them do wrong.
3. Organization:
   List on the board with the children the things we ask St. Michael for in our new prayer.
4. Broader Appreciation:
   The children dramatize the story of St. Michael.
5. Suggested Activity:
   The children illustrate the story of the fall of the bad angels.

LESSON PLAN FOR THE FEAST OF THE HOLY ROSARY

I. SUBJECT MATTER

Feast of the Holy Rosary

II. TYPE

Development

III. OBJECTIVES

A. To develop a proper understanding of the rosary.
B. To foster devotion to the Queen of the Holy Rosary.
C. To grow in love for Mary and her rosary.

IV. MATERIALS

Mysteries of the Rosary, Text, p. 9.
Poem — "Our Lady's Rosary," Sister Josita Belger, *Sing a Song of Holy Things*, p. 15.

V. PROCEDURE

A. Approach

Hold up a rosary. Question the children as to what it is, how we say it.

B. Presentation

1. Explanation and discussion:
   a) Describe the rosary, its mechanical form, and the prayers of which it is composed.

b) Tell the story of the origin of the Feast of the Holy Rosary.
   c) Discuss some incidents to illustrate the great power of the rosary.
   d) Discuss the times when the children and their families should say the rosary; discuss the need for frequent recitation of the rosary.
   e) Discuss the practice of carrying a rosary on our person.
   f) Discuss the parts of the rosary.
   g) Using the mysteries given in the children's text, begin teaching the mysteries and the correct recitation of the rosary. (Continue incidental teaching of the mysteries during the month of October.)
2. Application:
   The children resolve to say the rosary often, especially with their family.
3. Organization:
   Draw a large rosary on the board; the children name the parts of the rosary and the prayers to be said on each part.
4. Broader Appreciation:
   Poem — "Our Lady's Rosary," Sister Josita Belger, *Sing a Song of Holy Things*, p. 15.
5. Assignment:
   The mysteries of the rosary.
6. Suggested Activity:
   The children build a large classroom rosary on the bulletin board, adding pictures and decades as each new mystery is developed.

CORRELATED ACTIVITIES FOR UNIT ONE

Art
1. The children illustrate in the form of a booklet, frieze, or picture, one of the poems taken in this unit.
2. The children draw a picture of the stone tablets on which were written the Ten Commandments.
3. The children draw a picture of a child going up the steps, "know, love, and serve" to heaven.
4. Picture Study: The Last Supper by Da Vinci.

Music
1. Hymns:
   a) Holy God, We Praise Thy Name, *St. Gregory Hymnal*, p. 39.
   b) Our Father, *People's Hymnal*, T-10.
   c) Jesus, My Lord, My God, My All, *St. Gregory Hymnal*, p. 53.
   d) O Sacrament Most Holy, to the tune of O Lord, I Am Not Worthy.
   e) Review the First Holy Communion hymns learned in Grade Two.

English
1. The children memorize one or more of the poems taken in this unit.
2. Group composition: "What I Must Do To Be Happy With God in Heaven Some Day."

Science
1. The children bring to school and examine leaves, flowers, insects, etc., that show the wisdom, goodness, and power of God.
2. Plan a science unit on animals.

UNIT TWO. WHO AND WHAT GOD IS

(Text, *God's Truths Help Us Live*, pp. 45–96)

(Revised Baltimore Catechism No. 1 [Confraternity] Questions 8 to 39.)

INTRODUCTORY MATERIALS

I. INTRODUCTION FOR THE TEACHER

In this Unit, the child will strive to gain a better understanding of God by a further study of the perfections of God and the mystery of the Blessed Trinity. He will also gain knowledge of the story of creation; the success or failure of the angels; the creation of the world; the creation, fall, and punishment of man. References will be made to God's purpose for creating all things. In presenting this material, the teacher will develop the pupils' knowledge according to their understanding.

II. OBJECTIVES OF THE UNIT

A. To gain an understanding of the perfections of God and the mystery of the Blessed Trinity.
B. To teach the Act of Faith.
C. To show how God the Creator made all things for a purpose.
D. To increase love for God through an appreciation of, and gratitude for, the gifts of creation.

III. SUBJECT MATTER

A. God is a spirit infinitely perfect.
   1. God is the Supreme Being.
   2. God is eternal.
   3. God is all-knowing.
   4. God is all-present.
   5. God is almighty.
B. In God there are three Divine Persons.
   1. The special names of these Persons.
   2. The special work of these Persons.
   3. The equality of these Persons.
C. God is the Creator of heaven and earth.
   1. God made all creatures out of nothing.
   2. God made all creatures for a purpose.
   3. God watches over all creatures with loving care.
D. God's chief creatures are angels and men.
   1. God made angels.
   2. God made man.
E. Trial and punishment of Adam and Eve.
   1. How their obedience was tested.
   2. How their disobedience was punished.
F. How we share in Adam and Eve's punishments.
G. Sins we commit because of Adam's sin (actual sin).
   1. Mortal sin.
   2. Venial sin.
H. How we overcome sin.

IV. TEACHER REFERENCES FOR UNIT TWO

1. Baierl, Rev. Joseph, *The Creed Explained*, pp. 68–131; 132–230.
2. Belger, *Sing a Song of Holy Things*, pp. 6, 9, 16, 17, 19, 21, 86.
3. Brennan, *For Heaven's Sake*, pp. 3–6, 18–21.
4. Brennan, *Going His Way*, pp. 36–39, 13–16.
5. Kelly, *Baltimore Catechism No. 1 With Dev.*, pp. 12–22, 23–39.
6. Lovasik, *Catechism Sketched*, pp. 7–10, 10–19.
7. Montani, *St. Gregory Hymnal*, No. 38, 112.
8. Thayer, *The Child on His Knees*, pp. 46, 62, 63, 117.

LESSON PLANS FOR UNIT TWO

I. Introduction to Unit Two

Who and What God Is. Text, p. 45

LESSON PLAN 24

I. SUBJECT MATTER
Who and What God Is

II. TYPE
Introduction to Unit

III. OBJECTIVES
A. To prepare the children for a new unit of work.
B. To instill in the children a desire to learn.
C. To stimulate the children to do good thinking.

IV. MATERIALS
Unit Two, p. 45, in the children's text.

V. PROCEDURE

A. Approach
Today we are going to find out more about God. Open your text to Unit Two, p. 45.

B. Presentation
1. Pictures:
   a) The children study the pictures found in Unit Two.
   b) A discussion of the pictures will follow.
   c) The children ask any questions they have.
2. Summary: The children summarize the things they will learn in this Unit.
   The children discuss why they want to learn these truths.

II. Work Study Periods for Unit Two
(Lesson Plans 25–55)

LESSON PLAN 25

> "I am Who am" (Exod. 3:14).
> Blackboard

UNIT TWO, PART 1, LESSON PLAN 25, God Is a Spirit Infinitely Perfect. Text, p. 46

I. SUBJECT MATTER
God Is an Infinitely Perfect Spirit, Supreme and Eternal

II. TYPE
Development

III. OBJECTIVES
A. To strengthen the children's idea of and belief in God.
B. To lead the children to show by actions that they believe in God.

IV. MATERIALS
Picture — Moses and the Burning Bush

V. PROCEDURE

A. Approach
Discuss: Did you ever see your soul? How do you know that there is such a thing as the soul?

B. Presentation
1. Explanation and discussion:
   a) Explain that God is not seen with our eyes, either, but yet we know that He lives because of what He does. Explain that God is a spirit; define the term: spirit.
      1) Approach the fact that God is a spirit with the story of Moses and the Burning Bush; show and discuss the picture.
   b) Explain that God is infinitely perfect; define the term "infinitely perfect." Give examples to show that God is infinitely perfect.
      1) We can't measure His goodness — He has more goodness than anyone in the world.
      2) We can't measure His mercy — He can forgive all sins, etc.
   c) Explain two of God's perfections:
      1) Recall that God is the Supreme Being (Catechism answer). Discuss why; discuss why there can be only one Supreme Being.
      2) Explain that God is eternal.
         (*a*) God has always lived; He was living long before He made the earth; God had to live forever or someone greater than He would have had to make Him and then He would not have been the Supreme Being.
         (*b*) God will live forever.
         (*c*) God will never change: give examples to show this; e.g., God was always infinitely good and will remain that way. He isn't good one day and bad the next as we are.
         (*d*) Refer again to the story of Moses — "I am Who am."
         (*e*) End presentation by repeating exact answers of the Revised Baltimore Catechism No. 1 (Confraternity), questions 8, 9, Text, pp. 86–87.

2. Application:
Will we, too, live forever? How? The children resolve to do little acts today to show God that they want to live forever with Him in heaven.

3. Organization:
   a) Can we see God?
   b) Why can't we see Him?
   c) When shall we see God?
   d) How perfect is God?
   e) What two perfections of God did we just talk about?

4. Broader Appreciation:
The children dramatize the story of Moses and the Burning Bush.

5. Assignment:
Catechism questions 8 and 9, at end of Unit Two in children's text.

6. Suggested Activity:
The children illustrate the story of Moses and the Burning Bush.

UNIT TWO, PART 1, (cont.). Text, p. 49

LESSON PLAN 26

> "God Sees Me."
> Blackboard

I. SUBJECT MATTER
God Is All-knowing and All-present

23

II. TYPE
Development

III. OBJECTIVES
A. To develop the knowledge that God knows and sees everything.
B. To arouse in the children a deep love for God who is all-present.
C. To better our thoughts and actions.

IV. MATERIALS
Story — "God's Secret," Brennan, *For Heaven's Sake*, pp. 3–6.

V. PROCEDURE

A. Approach
Discuss: How many of you have ever seen a telescope? What is it? Why is it like a big eye? Explain that today we are going to learn how God, the infinitely perfect Being, knows all things and is present everywhere.

B. Presentation
1. Explanation and Discussion:
   a) Explain that God sees all that is going on in the world at every minute. He knows everything we do, everything we say, He even knows our most secret thoughts.
      1) The children give examples of some of the things that God knows right now.
      2) Discuss God's happiness in seeing us do good, and His anger in seeing us do wrong.
   b) Explain that if God knows everything that is going on in the world at every minute, then He knows everything that all His children do, think, and say. Discuss: Explain that God is so great that He remembers everything that has ever happened here on the earth.
      1) The children give examples of some things that God must remember about the past.
   c) Explain that God is so great that He not only knows what has happened and is happening right now, but He also knows what is going to happen in the future.
      1) The children give examples of some of the things about their future that God already knows.
   d) Discuss: If God knows everything that is going on in the world right now, then where is God? Why can't we see Him? Define the term: all-present; give examples to show that God is everywhere.
   e) Discuss: Why does God want to be all over the world at every minute, knowing everything that goes on? (Stress God's loving Providence.)
   f) End presentation by repeating exact words of the Revised Baltimore Catechism No. 1 (Confraternity) questions 10, 11, 12, Text, p. 87.
2. Application:
   The children resolve to be conscious of God's presence throughout the day and to do only the things that please Him.
3. Organization:
   a) Group composition: God sees all things. God hears all things. God knows all things. God is everywhere.
4. Broader Appreciation:
   Story — "God's Secret," Brennan, *For Heaven's Sake*, pp. 3–6.
5. Assignment:
   Catechism questions 10, 11, and 12, p. 87.
6. Suggested Activity:
   The children practice writing the group composition just composed.

UNIT TWO, PART 1 (cont.). Text, p. 49

LESSON PLAN 27

> "The winds and seas obey him" (Mt. 8:27).
> Blackboard

I. SUBJECT MATTER
God Is Almighty

II. TYPE
Development

III. OBJECTIVES
A. To develop further the knowledge of the almighty power of God.
B. To instill in the children a deep reverence for God and gratitude to Him for keeping them in existence.
C. To instill in the children the desire to know God better so as to love Him more.

IV. MATERIALS
Poem — "God's Greatness," Sister Josita Belger, *Sing a Song of Holy Things*, p. 9.

V. PROCEDURE

A. Approach
Can anyone in this room make it rain today? Why not? Can we make the wind blow? Why not?

B. Presentation
1. Explanation and discussion:
   a) Discuss some of the things we can do and some things that we cannot do because they are too hard or impossible for us to do.
   b) Explain that God can do all things: nothing is hard or impossible for Him. Explain the proposition: God is almighty.
   c) Teacher and pupils give examples to show that God is almighty:
      1) God made the earth out of nothing.

2) Only God can keep the stars in the sky.
3) God can make the rain fall and the wind blow.
- d) Recall the story of Jesus stopping the storm.
- e) End the presentation by repeating exact answers of Revised Baltimore Catechism No. 1 (Confraternity), question 13, Text, p. 87.
2. Application:
Many things are hard for us to do, aren't they? We couldn't even move a finger if almighty God didn't give us the power to do so. We couldn't even be good if God wouldn't give us the help to be good. The children resolve to ask God for His help when they need it.
3. Organization:
- a) God is the Supreme Being.
- b) God is all-knowing.
- c) God is all-present.
- d) God is almighty.
4. Broader Appreciation:
Poem — "God's Greatness," Sister Josita Belger, *Sing a Song of Holy Things*, p. 9.
5. Assignment:
Catechism question 13, p. 87, at end of Unit Two in children's text.
6. Suggested Activity:
The children compose a prayer to acknowledge God's almighty power.

UNIT TWO, PART 1 (cont.). Text, p. 49

LESSON PLAN 28

The children read or reread and discuss Part 1, p. 46 in their text.

UNIT TWO, PART 2, LESSON PLANS 29–31, The Blessed Trinity. Text, p. 51

LESSON PLAN 29

"O Most Holy Trinity, I adore Thee" (Raccolta, 12).
Blackboard

I. SUBJECT MATTER
The Blessed Trinity

II. TYPE
Development

III. OBJECTIVES
A. To develop further the idea of the Blessed Trinity.
B. To arouse in the children a holy reverence for God.
C. To incite in the children a desire to honor the Blessed Trinity with reverence and devotion.

IV. MATERIALS
Poem — "Blessed Trinity," Sister Josita Belger, *Sing a Song of Holy Things*, p. 6.

V. PROCEDURE

A. Approach
Make the Sign of the Cross aloud. Whose names do we say when we make the Sign of the Cross? Who are these persons?

B. Presentation
1. Explanation and discussion:
   - a) Recall and discuss the mystery of the Blessed Trinity:
     1) The names of the three Persons in God
     2) Symbols of the Blessed Trinity
        (a) Tell briefly the story of St. Patrick and the shamrock.
     3) The special work of each Person:
        (a) God the Father — Creator
        (b) God the Son — Redeemer
        (c) God the Holy Ghost — Sanctifier
     4) The equality of these Persons
     5) Evidence for this mystery
        (a) The story of the baptism of Jesus.
        (b) "There are three who give testimony in heaven."
     6) The special dwelling place of the Blessed Trinity (in our souls).
   - b) Explain that each Sunday is dedicated to the Blessed Trinity.
   - c) Discuss known prayers in honor of the Blessed Trinity.
     1) "Sign of the Cross"
     2) "Glory Be"
     3) "Apostles' Creed"
   - d) End presentation by repeating exact words of the Revised Baltimore Catechism No. 1 (Confraternity), questions 14, 15, 16, Text, pp. 87–88.
2. Application:
The children resolve to honor the Blessed Trinity dwelling in them by often reciting the prayer, Glory be . . .
3. Organization:
Elicit from the children the facts they know about the Blessed Trinity. Write each statement on the board.
4. Broader Appreciation:
Poem: "Blessed Trinity," Sister Josita Belger, *Sing a Song of Holy Things*, p. 6.
5. Assignment:
Catechism Questions 14, 15, and 16, pp. 87–88, at end of Unit Two in children's text.
6. Suggested Activity:
Symbols of the Blessed Trinity.

UNIT TWO, PART 2 (cont.).

LESSON PLAN 30

> "I believe in one God" (Credo of the Mass).
> Blackboard

I. **SUBJECT MATTER**
Act of Faith

II. **TYPE**
Development

III. **OBJECTIVES**
A. To teach the Act of Faith.
B. To show a strong faith in God and in the truths that the Catholic Church teaches.
C. To recite this prayer with attention and devotion.

IV. **MATERIALS**
Prayer — The Act of Faith, p. 3 in children's text.

V. **PROCEDURE**

A. **Approach**
Would you like to learn a new prayer that will help you tell God that you believe in the Blessed Trinity?

B. **Presentation**
1. Explanation and discussion:
   a) Recite slowly and devoutly the "Act of Faith" while the children listen.
   b) Explain and discuss the prayer, phrase by phrase.
   c) Begin memorization of the prayer.
2. Application:
   The children promise to learn the prayer well so that they can recite it with attention and devotion.
3. Organization:
   List on the board with the children the things they tell God they believe when they recite this prayer.
4. Broader Appreciation:
   The children slowly and devoutly read the new prayer from their text.
5. Assignment:
   Prayer — "Act of Faith," p. 3, in Text.
6. Suggested Activity:
   The children may write the Act of Faith.

UNIT TWO, PART 2 (cont.).

LESSON PLAN 31

The children read or reread and discuss Part 2, p. 51, in their text.

UNIT TWO, PART 3, LESSON PLANS 32–33.
Text, p. 55

LESSON PLAN 32

> "Praise Him, sun and moon; praise Him, all you shining stars" (Ps. 148.3).
> Blackboard

I. **SUBJECT MATTER**
God Made the World

II. **TYPE**
Development

III. **OBJECTIVES**
A. To develop further the truth that God is the Creator of heaven and earth.
B. To develop the idea that God made all things for a purpose.
C. To create in the children an attitude of dependence upon God.
D. To lead the children to act always in a manner befitting a creature of God.

IV. **MATERIALS**
Hymn, "O God of Loveliness," Montani, *St. Gregory Hymnal*, No. 38, p. 58.

V. **PROCEDURE**

A. **Approach**
Discuss the things that we would need in order to make a small gift box for someone that we love.

B. **Presentation**
1. Explanation and discussion:
   a) Explain that God the Father also made something for someone He loved: He made the world for His children. Discuss: What did God need to make the world? Explain that God had to will or wish it and the things that He wanted were made. Recall that God could do this because He is almighty. The children name things that God made. Recall the terms: Creator, creation, creature.
   b) Recall the fact that God is the Supreme Being:
      1) God is greater than all the things that He made.
      2) All things belong to God.
      3) God may do as He pleases with the things that He made.
   c) Explain and discuss God's purpose for Creation:
      1) God made His creatures to praise Him.
         (a) By existing (all creation).
         (b) By giving light (sun, moon, stars).
         (c) By being beautiful (all creation).

(d) By living (angels, men, animals, birds, fish, plants).
(e) By thinking and being free (angels and men).
(f) By showing His goodness and greatness.

2) God made some creatures to share His happiness:
(a) Angels
(b) Men
(1) Explain that only angels and men can share God's happiness because they are the only creatures who have spiritual faculties, a mind and a will, making them truly "images" of God.

d) Discuss: Since God made the world, and all things belong to Him, do you think He takes care of His creatures? How can you tell? The children give examples to show how God takes care of the things that He made. Compare God's tender care of the things He made with the loving care of good earthly fathers toward their children.

e) End the presentation by repeating exact words of the Revised Baltimore Catechism No. 1 (Confraternity), questions 17–18, Text, p. 88.

2. Organization:
a) How do you know that all the things in heaven and on earth belong to God?
b) How do you know that God didn't forget about His creatures after He made them?
c) For what two reasons did God make His creatures?

3. Application:
The children suggest ways in which they show that all the things that God made belong to Him. The children suggest ways in which they can show God every day that they belong to Him.

4. Broader Appreciation:
Hymn — "O God of Loveliness," Montani, *St. Gregory Hymnal*, No. 38, p. 58.

5. Assignment:
Catechism questions 17 and 18, p. 88, at the end of Unit Two in children's text.

6. Suggested Activity:
The children draw pictures of some of God's creatures.

UNIT TWO, PART 3 (cont.).

LESSON PLAN 33

The children read or reread and discuss Part 3, p. 55, in their text.

UNIT TWO, PART 4, LESSON PLANS 34–37, God Made the Angels. Text, p. 57

LESSON PLAN 34

"Bless the Lord, all you His Angels" (Raccolta, 441).
Blackboard

I. SUBJECT MATTER
The Creation and Fall of the Angels

II. TYPE
Development

III. OBJECTIVES
A. To develop further the children's understanding of the creation, the test, and reward or punishment of the angels.
B. To lead the children to practice obedience.
C. To instill in the children respect for God's authority.

IV. MATERIALS
Picture — St. Michael and the Bad Angels.

V. PROCEDURE

A. Approach
Discuss: Who are the chief creatures of God? Which of the two is greater? What are angels?

B. Presentation
1. Explanation and discussion:
a) Explain that angels are created spirits without bodies. Define the terms.
b) Explain and discuss why God made the angels:
1) To praise Him.
2) To share His happiness.
c) Explain and discuss the great gifts that God gave to the angels:
1) They were filled with grace.
2) They would never die.
3) Great minds.
4) Free will (define term).
5) Great power and strength.
d) Tell vividly and by means of a chalk talk the story of the trial and fall of the angels. Explain and discuss the reward or punishment given to the angels and God's justice in giving them only one chance.
e) End the presentation by repeating exact words of the Revised Baltimore Catechism No. 1 (Confraternity), questions 19–21, Text, p. 88.

2. Application:
Why did the bad angels fall? Why do we fall into sin? The children resolve to obey always as the good angels did, even if it is hard to do the right thing.

3. Organization:
   a) What are angels?
   b) Why did God make the angels?
   c) What gifts did God give to the angels?
   d) How did God test the angels?
   e) What happened to the angels who obeyed God?
   f) What happened to the angels who disobeyed God?
   g) Who was the leader of the good angels?
   h) Who was the leader of the bad angels?
4. Broader Appreciation:
   The children recite the prayer, "Bless the Lord, all you His angels."
5. Assignment:
   Catechism questions 19, 20, and 21, p. 88, at the end of Unit Two in children's text.
6. Suggested Activity:
   The children practice writing the prayer to St. Michael, p. 7 in their text.

UNIT TWO, PART 4 (cont.).

LESSON PLAN 35

The children read or reread and discuss Part 4, p. 57, in their text.

UNIT TWO, PART 4 (cont.). Text, p. 59

LESSON PLAN 36

> "All you angels and archangels, pray for us" (Raccolta, 687).
>
> **Blackboard**

I. SUBJECT MATTER
The Good Angels

II. TYPE
Development

III. OBJECTIVES
A. To develop an understanding of the work of the good and bad angels.
B. To lead the children to listen to the inspiration of their Guardian Angels.
C. To lead the children to practice devotion to God's holy angels.

IV. MATERIALS
Pictures of good angels. Story: "Nuggins," Brennan, *Going His Way*, pp. 13–16.

V. PROCEDURE
A. Approach
Review briefly yesterday's story of the fall of the bad angels.

B. Presentation
1. Explanation and discussion:
   a) Discuss the great reward that the good angels received for their obedience to God.
   b) Show pictures and explain the work of the good angels:
      1) They adore and praise God eternally.
      2) Some pray to God for us.
      3) Some act as messengers (discuss messages of Gabriel).
      4) Some act as Guardian Angels.
         (a) Discuss the work of our Guardian Angels; show pictures; discuss.
         (b) Discuss God's goodness in giving us an angel.
         (c) The children tell of incidents in their lives where their angel helped them.
         (d) Tell briefly the incident in the life of Tobias when his Guardian Angel helped him.
         (e) Review the prayer: "Angel of God."
         (f) End the presentation by repeating exact words of the Revised Baltimore Catechism No. 1 (Confraternity), questions 22, 23, Text, p. 89.
2. Application:
   a) Of all the angels of God, which should you love the best? Why? How often should you think of your Guardian Angel? How often should you pray to him? How can you please your Guardian Angel today?
3. Organization:
   List on the board with the children the times when they need their Guardian Angels' help the most.
4. Broader Appreciation:
   Story — "Nuggins," Brennan, *Going His Way*, pp. 13–16.
5. Assignment:
   Catechism questions 22 and 23, p. 89, at the end of Unit Two, in children's text.
6. Suggested Activity:
   The children draw pictures of themselves being helped by their Guardian Angels during the day.

UNIT TWO, PART 5, Guardian Angels. Text, p. 61

LESSON PLAN 37

I. SUBJECT MATTER
God Made the World; God Made Angels

II. TYPE
Discussion

III. OBJECTIVES
A. To lead the children to a better understanding and appreciation of the subject studied.

B. To lead the children to apply to daily living the truths learned in this part of the Unit.

IV. MATERIALS
Children's text, Unit Two, Parts 3, 4, and 5, pp. 55–63.

V. PROCEDURE

A. Approach
Today we are going to talk about God our Creator and the angels He created. Let us see how much we know.

B. Presentation
1. Set up standards for the discussion.
   a) The children help formulate a few rules to be followed while carrying on this discussion.
   b) Teacher writes rules on the board.
2. Present for discussion the material found in Unit Two, Parts 3, 4, and 5, pp. 55–63, in the children's text.
3. Generalization:
   The children give some important points in the form of statements which they wish to remember as a conclusion of this discussion.
   End the presentation by repeating exact words of the Revised Baltimore Catechism No. 1, questions 17–23, Text, pp. 88, 89.
4. Application:
   The children formulate resolutions resulting from the discussion.
5. Assignment:
   Review Catechism questions 17–23, pp. 88–89, at the end of Unit Two in children's text.

UNIT TWO, PARTS 4 AND 5 (cont.)

LESSON PLAN 38

The children read or reread and discuss Parts 4 & 5, pp. 57–63, in their text.

UNIT TWO, PART 6, LESSON PLANS 39–42, Our First Parents and Their Sin. Text, p. 63

LESSON PLAN 39

> "Let the earth bless the Lord . . ." (Dan. 3:10).
> Blackboard

I. SUBJECT MATTER
The Creation of the World for Man

II. TYPE
Development

III. OBJECTIVES
A. To develop the knowledge of the order of and the creation of the world.

B. To instill in the children a greater appreciation of God's gifts.
C. To teach gratitude toward God for all His gifts.

IV. MATERIALS
Poem, "Words," Thayer, *The Child on His Knees*, pp. 62–63.

V. PROCEDURE

A. Approach
Discuss: Do you think that God was disappointed when all the angels did not get to share His happiness with Him?

B. Presentation
1. Explanation and discussion:
   a) Explain that God could have made more angels, but didn't want to. Instead, He wanted to make another kind of creature — man. Explain that man is not as great as the angels, but he is greater than all the other things that God made.
   b) Explain that man was made some place out of heaven; there God tested him to see if he deserved heaven. Explain that God made this place very beautiful; He made everything in it first, then made man.
   c) Give a chalk talk on Creation; discuss God's purpose for making each thing, and man's use of these things; teach the symbol for Creation.
2. Organization:
   The children list on the board with the teacher the works of Creation.
3. Application:
   Do you think that God showed great love for man by making such a beautiful world in which man could live? How can we best thank God for His gifts? (By taking care of them and sharing them with others.) The children resolve to thank God always for His great gifts to us.
4. Broader Appreciation:
   Poem — "Words," Thayer, *The Child on His Knees*, pp. 62, 63.
5. Assignment:
   None.
6. Suggested Activity:
   The children make a frieze of the works of creation.

UNIT TWO, PART 6 (cont.). Text, p. 64

LESSON PLAN 40

> "My God, I give Thee thanks for what Thou givest" (Raccolta, 9).
> Blackboard

I. **SUBJECT MATTER**
God Makes Man

II. **TYPE**
Development

III. **OBJECTIVES**
A. To develop the understanding of God's great gifts to man.
B. To instill in the children an attitude of greater love toward God.
C. To lead the children to use God's personal gifts well.

IV. **MATERIALS**
Large picture of Adam and Eve in the garden.

V. **PROCEDURE**

A. **Approach**
Review briefly the work of Creation. Explain that today we are going to talk about the greatest creatures that God put on this earth.

B. **Presentation**
1. Explanation and discussion:
   a) Tell vividly the story of the creation of Adam and Eve; show the picture; discuss man's privilege of ruling over and using all the things of the earth for himself.
   b) Explain that God gave man great gifts:
      1) A beautiful body that would never get sick or die.
      2) A wonderful mind.
      3) Free will to choose right or wrong.
         (a) God made man's will so strong that it would be easy for him to be good.
      4) Easy work, plenty of food, a beautiful place in which to live, etc.
      5) God gave man a soul that would live forever, a soul made to His likeness and image.
      6) God gave the best gift of all — grace, which made us children of God, sharing in God's own life. Explain that this was man's greatest gift from God.
   c) Explain the Catechism question, What is man?
   d) Explain that these gifts were to be given to everyone born into this world if Adam obeyed God; recall the command that God gave not to eat of the forbidden fruit.
   e) End the presentation by repeating exact words of the Revised Baltimore Catechism No. 1 (Confraternity), questions 24, 25, 26, Text, p. 89.
2. Application:
   Wasn't God good to Adam and Eve? Which was the greatest gift that Adam and Eve received from God? Did Adam and Eve lose this great gift? The children resolve never to lose this gift from God as Adam and Eve did.
3. Organization:
   List on the board with the children the special gifts that God gave to man.
4. Broader Appreciation:
   The children repeat the ejaculation given at the top of this plan.
5. Assignment:
   Catechism questions 24, 25, 26, p. 89, at end of Unit Two in the text.
6. Suggested Activity:
   The children draw a picture of Adam and Eve living in the Garden of Paradise.

UNIT TWO, PART 6 (cont.). Text, p. 65

LESSON PLAN 41

"Let all Thy creatures serve Thee" (Judith 16:17).
Blackboard

I. **SUBJECT MATTER**
The Fall of Adam and Eve

II. **TYPE**
Development

III. **OBJECTIVES**
A. To develop the understanding of the consequences of Adam and Eve's disobedience to God.
B. To show the children God's infinite goodness and mercy in giving man another chance.
C. To lead the children to practice the virtue of obedience.

IV. **MATERIALS**
Picture — Adam and Eve Leaving the Garden.
Poem — "Excuses," Thayer, *The Child on His Knees*, p. 117.

V. **PROCEDURE**

A. **Approach**
Recall the wonderful gifts that Adam and Eve received from God. Also recall God's command to them. They were to be tested.

B. **Presentation**
1. Explanation and discussion:
   a) Tell vividly the story of the fall of Adam and Eve and their flight from the Garden. Show picture and discuss.
   b) List the punishments that Adam and Eve received from God and explain:
      1) All their grace was taken away.
      2) Heaven was closed to all men.
      3) Their bodies would have to suffer and die.
      4) They would have to work hard.
      5) Their minds were darkened.
      6) Their wills were weakened.

c) Discuss: Do you think Adam and Eve were sorry that they had disobeyed God? Contrast the reward they would have received for obedience with the punishment they received for disobedience.

d) Discuss: Why was God right and just in punishing Adam and Eve so terribly? Do you think God still loved them? Explain that in our next Unit we will learn about a wonderful promise that God made to show that He still loved Adam and Eve and all men.

e) End the presentation by repeating exact words of the Revised Baltimore Catechism No. 1 (Confraternity), questions 27, 28, Text, pp. 89, 90.

2. Application:
Do we ever disobey God? The children resolve to try to obey God perfectly today.

3. Organization:
List with the children the punishments Adam and Eve received for their sin.

4. Broader Appreciation:
Poem — "Excuses," Thayer, *The Child on His Knees*, p. 117.

5. Assignment:
Catechism questions 27 and 28, pp. 89–90, at the end of Unit Two.

6. Suggested Activity:
The children write a paragraph to show that God was just in punishing Adam and Eve.

UNIT TWO, PART 6 (cont.). Text, p. 63

LESSON PLAN 42

The children read or reread and discuss Part 6, p. 63, in their text.

UNIT TWO, PART 7, LESSON PLANS 43–45, Adam's Sin Makes Us Suffer. Text, p. 67

LESSON PLAN 43

> "The Father Himself loveth you" (Jn. 17:27).
> Blackboard

I. SUBJECT MATTER
We Suffer Because of Adam's Sin

II. TYPE
Development

III. OBJECTIVES
A. To give an understanding of how we suffer because of Adam's sin.
B. To lead the children to appreciate God's love and mercy.
C. To inspire greater love for and trust in God.

IV. MATERIALS
Picture — Immaculate Conception.
Poem: "So Much," Thayer, *The Child on His Knees*, p. 101.

V. PROCEDURE

A. Approach
Recall God's punishment of Adam and Eve, and the mercy He showed to them.

B. Presentation

1. Explanation and discussion:
   a) Explain that Adam and Eve's sin was great and that all of their children would have to suffer because of it.
   b) List the punishments and explain each.
      1) We are born without sanctifying grace, with original sin on our souls; explain term: original sin.
      2) Our bodies must suffer and die; discuss various kinds of suffering.
      3) Our minds are darkened — it is hard for us to know right from wrong; have to study.
      4) Our wills are weakened — it is hard for us to choose good, easy to choose bad.
      5) We have to work hard.
   c) Discuss Mary's privilege in being free from original sin. Show picture and discuss.
   d) Explain that our punishments are great, but God loves us and wants to help us. List ways in which God helps us overcome these punishments:
      1) Baptism takes away original sin and gives us sanctifying grace.
      2) Suffering can be made a means of making up for sin.
      3) Our bodies will rise again at the end of the world. (Do not go into detail.)
      4) God's grace enlightens our minds and strengthens our wills.
      5) Work can be turned into a prayer.
   e) End the presentation by repeating exact words of the Revised Baltimore Catechism No. 1 (Confraternity), questions 29–32, Text, p. 90.

2. Application:
The children resolve to rely upon God for His help whenever they need it.

3. Organization:
List with the children our punishments and the helps God gives to overcome them.

4. Broader Appreciation:
Poem — "So Much," Thayer, *The Child on His Knees*.

5. Assignment:
Catechism questions 29, 30, 31, and 32, p. 90, at the end of Unit Two in the children's text.
6. Suggested Activity:
The children find or draw pictures of things that happen to us today because of Adam's sin.

UNIT TWO, PART 7 (cont.).

LESSON PLAN 44

The children read or reread and discuss Part 7, p. 67, in their text.

UNIT TWO, PART 7 (cont.).

LESSON PLAN 45

I. SUBJECT MATTER
Creation and Fall

II. TYPE
Discussion

III. MATERIALS
Children's text, Unit Two, Parts 6 and 7, pp. 63, 70.

IV. PROCEDURE
See plan for discussion found in Unit One, Lesson 8 in Manual, p. 13.

UNIT TWO, PART 8, LESSON PLANS 46, 47, Actual Sin. Text, p. 70

LESSON PLAN 46

> "O God, be merciful to me, the sinner" (Raccolta, 14).
>
> Blackboard

I. SUBJECT MATTER
Actual Sin

II. TYPE
Development

III. OBJECTIVES
A. To develop a further understanding of what sin is.
B. To instill hatred for sin in the hearts of the children.
C. To lead the children to obey God's laws perfectly.

IV. MATERIALS
Poem — "Why Do You Care," Thayer, *The Child on His Knees*, p. 46.

V. PROCEDURE

A. Approach
What is the worst thing in the whole world? What kept the angels out of heaven? Why did God take some of Adam's wonderful gifts away?

B. Presentation
1. Explanation and discussion:
   a) Explain the meaning of the word; sin, discuss.
   b) Refer to the first sin committed on this earth — from it comes original sin. Explain that we don't commit original sin, but it is on our souls when we are born.
   c) Explain that there is a sin which we ourselves commit — actual sin.
      1) Explain what actual sin is.
      2) Give examples of willful thoughts, desires, words, actions, and omissions against God's laws; the children give examples.
   d) Explain that sometimes an actual sin is a great offense against God's law and sometimes it is a less offense — both offend God, both hurt our souls. Give the names of these two kinds of actual sin — mortal and venial. Explain that in our next lessons we will learn about mortal sin and venial sin.
   e) Discuss: Can you think of anyone who never committed an actual sin? Recall that Mary was free from all sin.
   f) End the presentation by repeating exact words of the Revised Baltimore Catechism No. 1 (Confraternity), questions 33, 34, Text, pp. 90, 91.
2. Application:
   If sin is such a terrible thing, what must we do about it? The children resolve to keep from sin today by asking Mary's help since she was free from all sin.
3. Organization:
   a) What is sin?
   b) How many kinds of sin are there?
   c) What is the name of the sin that we inherit from Adam?
   d) What is the name of the sins we commit?
   e) How many kinds of actual sin are there?
4. Assignment:
   Catechism questions 33 and 34, pp. 90, 91, at the end of Unit Two in the children's text.
5. Suggested Activity:
   Writing lesson — "O Mary conceived without sin . . ."

UNIT TWO, PART 8 (cont.).

LESSON PLAN 47

The children read or reread and discuss Part 8, p. 70, in the children's text.

UNIT TWO, PART 9, LESSON PLANS 48—49, Mortal Sin. Text, p. 74

LESSON PLAN 48

> "My Mother, deliver me from mortal sin" (Raccolta, 297).
>
> Blackboard

I. **SUBJECT MATTER**
Mortal Sin

II. **TYPE**
Development

III. **OBJECTIVES**
A. To give the children a knowledge of what mortal sin is.
B. To inspire trust in God's infinite mercy.
C. To lead the children to avoid mortal sin as the worst evil in the world.

IV. **MATERIALS**
None

V. **PROCEDURE**

A. Approach
If you were given your choice of having to die or committing a mortal sin, which would you choose? Why?

B. Presentation
1. Explanation and discussion:
   a) Explain what a mortal sin is; explain what the word mortal means.
   b) Explain and discuss what mortal sin does to us.
      1) It takes away the life of grace.
      2) It takes away our right to heaven.
      3) It makes us God's enemy.
   c) Compare a soul in mortal sin with a piece of dead wood good only to burn.
   d) Explain what is necessary to make a sin mortal.
      1) It must be a serious sin.
      2) We must know it is a big sin.
      3) We must want to do it.
   e) Explain how mortal sin can be forgiven:
      1) By a good confession.
      2) By an act of perfect contrition.
   f) Explain and discuss how mortal sin can be avoided:
      1) By using the sacraments of penance and Holy Eucharist often.
      2) By avoiding the habit of venial sins . . . staying away from all sin.
      3) By staying away from the occasions of sin.
   g) End the presentation by repeating exact answers of the Revised Baltimore Catechism No. 1 (Confraternity), questions 35–37, Text, p. 91.

2. Application:
What is the only thing that can keep us out of heaven? The children resolve to hate mortal sin and *never* to commit it — it sometimes looks good to us. The children resolve to make an act of perfect contrition if ever they fall into mortal sin; then, go to confession.

3. Organization:
   a) What is a mortal sin?
   b) What does mortal sin do to us?
   c) What three things are necessary to make a sin mortal?
   d) How can you stay away from mortal sin?

4. Broader Appreciation:
The children make up a group prayer, asking God to keep them from mortal sin.

5. Assignment:
Catechism questions 35, 36, and 37, p. 91, at the end of Unit Two in children's text.

6. Suggested Activity:
The children practice writing the prayer just composed.

UNIT TWO, PART 9 (cont.).

LESSON PLAN 49

Children read or reread and discuss Part 9, p. 74, in their text.

UNIT TWO, PART 10, LESSON PLANS 50, 51, Venial Sin. Text, p. 78

LESSON PLAN 50

I. **SUBJECT MATTER**
Venial Sin

II. **TYPE**
Development

III. **OBJECTIVES**
A. To develop an understanding of venial sin.
B. To create an attitude of hatred toward all sin.
C. To lead the children to avoid frequent venial sin.

IV. **MATERIALS**
Poem — "Sin," Sister Josita Belger, *Sing a Song of Holy Things*, p. 86.

V. **PROCEDURE**

A. Approach
Briefly review mortal sin.

B. Presentation
1. Explanation and discussion:
   a) Explain what venial sin is.

b) Explain what it does to us:
     1) It weakens us in our resistance to evil.
     2) It keeps us from loving God and being loved as we should.
     3) It keeps us from getting as much grace as we should receive.
     4) It brings punishment on us.
  c) Explain how venial sin can be taken away:
     1) By confession.
     2) By prayer.
  d) Explain and discuss how venial sin can be avoided:
     1) By avoiding the occasions of sin.
     2) By bravely resisting temptations.
     3) By frequent use of the sacraments.
     4) By often thinking of God and how good He is.
  e) Give a chalk talk to illustrate the difference between a mortal sin and a venial sin.
  f) End the presentation by repeating exact words of the Revised Baltimore Catechism No. 1 (Confraternity), questions 38, 39, Text, p. 91.
2. Application:
   Must we try to keep away from venial sin? Why? The children resolve frequently to recall God's holy presence in them so that they will not displease the God of love.
3. Organization:
   Make with the children a list of sins that are usually mortal and a list of sins that are usually venial. (This will aid the children in keeping from thinking that "everything is a mortal sin.")
4. Broader Appreciation:
   Poem — "Sin," Sister Josita Belger, *Sing a Song of Holy Things*, p. 86.
5. Assignment:
   Catechism questions 38 and 39, p. 91, at the end of Unit Two in the children's text.
6. Suggested Activity:
   The children make up a very short composition on "Why I Should Hate Venial Sin."

UNIT TWO, PART 10 (cont.).

LESSON PLAN 51

Children read or reread and discuss Part 10, p. 78, in their text.

UNIT TWO, PART 11, LESSON PLANS 52–55, How to Practice Virtue. Text, p. 82

LESSON PLAN 52

> "Keep us this day without sin, O Lord" (Raccolta, 21).
>
> Blackboard

I. **SUBJECT MATTER**
   How to Practice Virtue

II. **TYPE**
   Development

III. **OBJECTIVES**
   A. To instill in the children a love and a desire for good acts.
   B. To lead the children to a practice of virtue.
   C. To develop the knowledge of how we can overcome sin.

IV. **MATERIALS**
   Story — "The Elephant and the Ants," Brennan, *Going His Way*, pp. 36–39.

V. **PROCEDURE**

   A. Approach
   We must be generous with God. We must strive to practice all those perfections which make us like to Him, and make us pleasing to Him — like Jesus and Mary.

   B. Presentation
   1. Explanation and discussion:
      a) Getting into the habit of doing things which will make us be like Christ is our great goal. Explain the term: habit. Explain that there are many ways to act like Christ:
         1) By prayer — especially the Mass.
         2) By receiving the sacraments.
         3) By avoiding the near occasions of sin.
         4) By using God's actual graces to perform works of mercy.
         5) By doing little penances — saying "no" to little things we want.
         6) By practicing the opposite virtues (good habits). List with the children some sins frequently committed by children and show the opposite virtue. Explain and discuss how these sins are overcome by practicing the opposite virtues.
      b) End the presentation by repeating exact words of the Revised Baltimore Catechism (Confraternity), No. 1, questions 32–39, Text, pp. 90–91.
   2. Organization:
      The children briefly review the ways to overcome sin.
   3. Application:
      Recall that every good act has a reward and every bad act has a punishment. Recall the reward of Abel and the punishment of Cain. The children resolve to overcome their bad habits by doing as many good acts each day as possible.
   4. Broader Appreciation:
      Story — "The Elephant and the Ants," Brennan, *Going His Way*, pp. 36–39.

5. Assignment:
Review Catechism questions 32–39, pp. 90–91, at the end of Unit Two in children's text.

6. Suggested Activity:
The children make a double picture; in the first, they show some child committing a sin; in the second, they show that child trying to overcome that bad habit.

UNIT TWO, PART 11 (cont.).

LESSON PLAN 53

The children read or reread and discuss Part 11, p. 82, in their text.

UNIT TWO, PART 11 (cont.).

LESSON PLAN 54

I. **SUBJECT MATTER**
"Problems"

II. **TYPE**
Discussion

III. **MATERIALS**
Children's text, p. 84 at the end of Unit Two.

IV. **PROCEDURE**
Same as discussion plan found in Unit One, Lesson 8, p. 13, in the Manual.

UNIT TWO, PART 11 (cont.).

LESSON PLAN 55

I. **SUBJECT MATTER**
God the Father Made All Things

II. **TYPE**
Drill

III. **MATERIALS**
Questions at the end of Unit Two, p. 92, in the children's text.

IV. **PROCEDURE**
Same as for drill lesson, Unit One, Lesson 21 in the Manual.

III. Culmination of Unit Two

LESSON PLAN 56

I. **SUBJECT MATTER**
God the Father Made All Things

II. **TYPE**
Culmination

III. **MATERIALS**
Hymns, poems, stories, etc., developed during this Unit.

IV. **PROCEDURE**
Same as for culmination plan, Unit One, Lesson 22 in the Manual.

IV. Evaluation of Unit Two

LESSON PLAN 57

The children take the written test found on pp. 94–96, at the end of Unit Two in their text.
After each Unit, reteach and retest where there are weaknesses revealed.

SPECIAL PLANS FOR THE LITURGICAL YEAR (Unit Two)

Last Sunday in October — Christ the King
"O Christ Jesus, I know You are the King of the world . . ." (*Raccolta*, 272)

*November 1 — All Saints
Prayer: "O God, Thou art all-powerful; make me a saint." (*Raccolta*, 15)

*November 2 — All Souls
Prayer: "Eternal rest grant unto them, O Lord." *Raccolta*, 582)

November 21 — Presentation of Mary
Prayer: "Holy Mary, pray for us." (*Raccolta*, 319)

*Thanksgiving Day — (Spiritual side)
Prayer: "My God, I give Thee thanks for what Thou givest." (*Raccolta*, 9)

Advent —
Prayer: "Come, O Lord, and tarry not." (*Raccolta*, 154)

December 3 — St. Francis Xavier
Prayer: "St. Francis Xavier, pray for us."

December 6 — St. Nicholas
Prayer: "St. Nicholas, help us by your loving kindness." (*Raccolta*, 550)

LESSON PLAN FOR THE FEAST OF ALL SAINTS

I. **SUBJECT MATTER**
Feast of All Saints
All Souls' Day

II. **TYPE**
Development

III. **OBJECTIVES**
A. To give the children a better understanding of these two great days.

To be developed thoroughly; lesson plans for each have been worked out and will be found on the following pages.

B. To inspire the children to imitate the virtues of the saints.
C. To foster devotion to the saints and to the poor souls.

IV. MATERIALS
Poem — "Feast of All Saints," *Sing a Song of Holy Things*, pp. 16–17.
Poem — "Feast of All Souls," *Sing a Song of Holy Things*, p. 19.

V. PROCEDURE

A. Approach
Two very important days are coming. Do you know what these two days are?

B. Presentation
1. Explanation and discussion:
   a) Explain the purpose of All Saints' Day; the children name some saints who have special feasts at this time; the children discuss the Blessed Virgin Mary as Queen of all Saints.
   b) Discuss: How did the saints become saints? How can we become a saint? How can we honor these saints? What do you know about your patron saint? Why do we have patron saints?
   c) Explain the purpose of the feast of All Souls; discuss the necessity for our praying for these souls; discuss the times when we should pray especially for the poor souls.
2. Application:
   The children suggest ways in which they wish to help the poor souls every day.
3. Organization:
   The children list the names of the two important coming days, and the things that they wish to do on these two days.
4. Broader Appreciation:
   Poems — "Feast of All Saints," and "Feast of All Souls Day," Sister Josita Belger, *Sing a Song of Holy Things*, pp. 16–17.
5. Suggested Activity:
   The children make and give a class report on their patron saint; put the report in a classroom book, "Our Patron Saints."

LESSON PLAN FOR THANKSGIVING DAY

I. SUBJECT MATTER
Thanksgiving Day Prayer: Morning Offering Prayer

II. TYPE
Development

III. OBJECTIVES
A. To give the children a better understanding of thanksgiving.
B. To teach the children a way of making every day a thanksgiving day.
C. To instill gratitude in the hearts of the children.

IV. MATERIALS
Poem — "Our Thanksgiving Day," Sister Josita Belger, *Sing a Song of Holy Things*, p. 21.

V. PROCEDURE

A. Approach
Discuss meaning of the term: Thanksgiving Day. Why celebrate?

B. Presentation
1. Explanation and discussion:
   a) Explain the origin and importance of this day.
   b) The children discuss the things they should thank God for; ways in which they can thank God for His gifts.
   c) Teach the "Morning Offering" as a way of making every minute of the day a prayer to God in thanksgiving for all His favors to us.
2. Application:
   The children resolve to thank God every day for His gifts.
3. Organization:
   List with the children the things that we should thank God for every day.
4. Broader Appreciation:
   Poem — "Our Thanksgiving Day."
5. Suggested Activity:
   Children compose original thank-you prayers.

CORRELATED ACTIVITIES FOR UNIT TWO

Art
1. The children illustrate the Unity and Trinity of God by designing a circle with a triangle within it.
2. The children make all-over patterns of circles or triangles.
3. The children make a Guardian Angel poster.
4. The children do stencil work on fruits and vegetables that God made.
5. The children draw pictures to illustrate the Bible stories taken in this Unit.

Music
1. Hymns:
   a) "O God of Loveliness," *St. Gregory Hymnal*, No. 38, p. 58.
   b) "Dear Angel! Ever at My Side," *St. Gregory Hymnal*, No. 112, p. 175.

English
1. The children dramatize any stories taken in this Unit.
2. The children memorize any poems taken in this Unit.
3. The children write original prayers, letters, or stories about topics of this Unit.

Science
1. The children begin a collection of living and non-living creatures of God.
2. Plan a science Unit on the earth; wind and air; plants and animals.

UNIT THREE. GOD THE SON BECAME MAN TO SAVE US

(Text, *God's Truths Help Us Live*, pp. 97–136)

(Revised Baltimore Catechism No. 1 [Confraternity] Questions 40–45.)

INTRODUCTORY MATERIAL

I. INTRODUCTION FOR THE TEACHER

This Unit considers the Incarnation, which is the coming of the Second Person of the Blessed Trinity in human flesh as the Saviour of all men. It begins with God's promise to send a Redeemer to fallen man, and continues with man's preparations for the Redeemer, the coming of the Redeemer, and His hidden life.

II. OBJECTIVES OF THE UNIT

A. To appreciate more fully God's fatherly love as shown to us in sending us the Redeemer.
B. To cultivate a deep feeling of gratitude to Jesus for showing us how to live.
C. To strive to imitate the virtues of Jesus, especially His obedience, kindness, and love of prayer.

III. SUBJECT MATTER

A. God prepares man for the Redeemer
 1. Promise made to Adam, Abraham, and King David
B. Man prepares for the Redeemer under the Old Law
 1. Man prepares by faith, sacrifice, prayer, and obedience
C. Fulfillment of the promise
 1. The Annunciation
 2. The Visitation
 3. The Birth of Our Lord
 4. The Adoration of the Shepherds
 5. The Presentation
 6. The Adoration of the Magi
 7. The Flight Into Egypt
 8. Life at Nazareth
D. Jesus is God made man

IV. TEACHER REFERENCES FOR UNIT THREE

1. Baierl, *The Creed Explained*, pp. 231–289.
2. Belger, *Sing a Song of Holy Things*, pp. 18, 27, 35.
3. Johnson, *The Bible Story*, pp. 111, 117, 141–161.
4. Lovasik, *The Catechism Sketched*, pp. 22–25.
5. *People's Hymnal*, A-1, A-5, R-15.
6. Thayer, *The Child on His Knees*, pp. 38, 49.

LESSON PLANS FOR UNIT THREE

I. Introduction to Unit Three

God the Son Became Man to Save Us. Text, p. 97

LESSON PLAN 58

I. SUBJECT MATTER
God the Son Became Man to Save Us

II. TYPE
Introduction

III. MATERIALS
Children's text, Unit Three, p. 97.

IV. PROCEDURE
Same as for introductory lesson for Unit Two, Lesson 24, p. 22, in Manual.

II. Work Study Periods for Unit Three
(Lesson Plans 59–83)

UNIT III, PARTS 1 AND 2, God Promised a Saviour to Adam.

God Makes His Promise to Others. Text, pp. 98–103

LESSON PLAN 59

> "Come O Lord, and tarry not" (Raccolta, 154).
> Blackboard

I. SUBJECT MATTER
God Promised a Saviour to Adam

II. TYPE
Development

III. OBJECTIVES
A. To gain a greater understanding of God's fatherly love for us in sending the Redeemer.
B. To become acquainted with the names of some people to whom God made the promise of the Redeemer known.
C. To show our gratitude to God for His goodness by saying prayers of thanksgiving and doing our best to please Him.

IV. MATERIALS
Poem: "The Life of Grace," Sister Josita Belger, *Sing a Song of Holy Things*, p. 18.

V. PROCEDURE

A. Approach
Do you know the promise that God made to Adam and Eve before He sent them out of the Garden of Paradise?

B. Presentation
1. Explanation and discussion:
   a) Explain God's promise of sending a Redeemer, and the necessity for His coming.
   b) Explain the terms: redeem, Redeemer, also the term: Saviour.
   c) Explain that Adam's sin was so great that it would take God to make satisfaction for the sin, therefore, God sent His Son.
   d) Explain that the Redeemer would not come at once — man would have to wait a long time for His coming.
   e) Explain that God made the promise of the Redeemer to others at different times — to Adam, Abraham, Moses, King David; discuss the reasons why God promised the Saviour to each.
   f) Explain that man hoped in God — trusted in God's promise.
   g) End the presentation by repeating exact answer to Revised Baltimore Catechism No. 1 (Confraternity), question 40, Text, p. 132.

2. Application:
   These people trusted God's word. They knew that God was taking care of them. Shall we not also place our trust in God and believe that He gives us many chances after we offend Him?

3. Organization:
   a) What promise did God make after Adam and Eve sinned?
   b) Who were some other people to whom God made the promise?
   c) What does the word "Redeemer" mean?
   d) How long did the people wait for the Redeemer?
   e) Why did God have to send His Son to be the Redeemer?

4. Broader Appreciation:
   Poem: "Life of Grace," Sister Josita Belger, *Sing a Song of Holy Things*, p. 18.

5. Assignment:
   Catechism question 40, p. 132, at end of Unit Three in children's texts.

6. Suggested Activity:
   The children make up original prayers of "Trust in God."

LESSON PLAN 60

The children read or reread and discuss Parts 1 and 2, pp. 98–103, in their texts.

UNIT THREE, PART 3, LESSON PLANS 61–64.
Man Prepares for the Redeemer. Text, p. 104

LESSON PLAN 61

> "Lord, increase our Faith" (Lk. 17:5)
> Blackboard

I. SUBJECT MATTER
Man Prepares for the Redeemer

II. TYPE
Development

III. OBJECTIVES
A. To gain a knowledge of how man prepared for the Redeemer by faith, prayer, and obedience.
B. To appreciate as far as possible the goodness and mercy of God to man even after man had continuously offended Him.
C. To increase the desire of preparing well at all times when receiving Holy Communion.

IV. MATERIALS
None

V. PROCEDURE

A. Approach
To whom did God make the promise of the Redeemer? Today we shall find out how man showed his belief in the promise and how he prepared for the coming of the Saviour.

B. Presentation
1. Explanation and discussion:
   a) Explain the fact that God wanted the people to remember always that the Redeemer would come some day. He expected them to prepare well for Him.
   b) Explain that God sent prophets to keep reminding the people of the Redeemer; explain the meaning of "Prophet."
   c) Explain and discuss that people were to get their hearts ready. Some did so by believing what God had taught. Cite some good ex-

amples of great faith in God — Noe, Abraham, Moses, King David.
    d) Explain that God also wanted His people to prepare in another way — prayer and obedience.
        1) People prayed over and over again for the Redeemer; Bible is filled with such prayers; give examples.
        2) God insisted also that people obey — they were rewarded or punished as they obeyed or disobeyed.
    e) Tell and discuss how these people prepared for the Saviour by their prayers and obedience — Moses and Israelites, King David, Simeon, Mary.
2. Application:
People prepared well for the coming of the Saviour. The children resolve to prepare well for each Holy Communion.
3. Organization:
Show how the people whom we have studied in this Unit prepared for the coming of the Redeemer by faith, sacrifice, prayer, and obedience.

Faith	*Prayer*	*Obedience*
King David	Abraham	King David
Abraham	Moses	Moses
Moses	Mary	Abraham
Mary		Mary

4. Broader Appreciation:
Children tell original stories of how God rewarded their obedience.
5. Assignment:
None
6. Suggested Activity:
The children draw pictures to illustrate ways in which people prepared for the Saviour's coming.

LESSON PLAN 62

UNIT THREE, PART 3 (cont.).

> "And when he had bound Isaac, his son, he laid him on the altar upon the pile of wood" (Gen. 22:9).
> Blackboard

I. SUBJECT MATTER
Man Prepares for the Saviour by Sacrifice

II. TYPE
Development

III. OBJECTIVES
A. To impart the knowledge that man prepared for the Saviour by offering sacrifice.
B. To gain an understanding of what a sacrifice is and of what it consists.
C. To develop a greater appreciation for Jesus' love and goodness shown to us by offering Himself on our altars daily during the Holy Sacrifice of the Mass.
D. To foster a spirit of making little sacrifices out of love for Jesus.

IV. MATERIALS
Pictures depicting the sacrifices offered by Abel, Noe, Abraham, or Melchisedech.

V. PROCEDURE

A. Approach
Recall briefly how people prepared for the coming of the Redeemer by faith, prayer, and obedience.

B. Presentation
1. Explanation and discussion:
    a) Explain that others prepared for the Redeemer by offering sacrifices.
        1) Explain what a sacrifice is and why it is offered. (Reserve explanation of four ends of sacrifice until Unit Five.)
        2) Explain essentials for every sacrifice: Priest-Victim-Altar.
        3) Tell and discuss how some people prepared for the Redeemer by offering their sacrifices to God: Abel, Noe, Abraham, Melchisedech, Israelites (Paschal Lamb).
    b) Explain how the Church prepares for the Saviour's coming each year during the holy season of Advent; discuss how we should keep Advent; discuss Advent sacrifices children can make.
2. Application:
The children make Advent resolutions.
3. Organization:
    a) What is a sacrifice?
    b) What is essential for offering sacrifice?
    c) Why were sacrifices offered to God?
    d) Name some sacrifices that some people offered.
4. Broader appreciation:
The children make up a little prayer in which they tell Jesus their Advent resolutions.
5. Assignment:
None
6. Suggested Activities:
    a) The children make a frieze of the sacrifices offered by some people of the Old Law.
    b) The children make posters showing sacrifices they can make during Advent.

UNIT THREE, PART 3 (cont.).

LESSON PLAN 63

The children read or reread and discuss Part 3, p. 104, in their text.

UNIT THREE, PART 3 (cont.).

LESSON PLAN 64

I. SUBJECT MATTER
Man Prepares for the Redeemer

II. TYPE
Discussion

III. MATERIALS
Children's text, Unit Three, Parts 1, 2, and 3, pp. 98–106.

IV. PROCEDURE
Same as for discussion plan in Unit One, Lesson 8, in the Manual, p. 13.

UNIT THREE, PARTS 4 AND 5, LESSON PLANS 65–67, God Keeps His Promise – The Annunciation.
Mary Visits Elizabeth. Text, pp. 107, 110

LESSON PLAN 65

> "And the word was made flesh and dwelt among us" (Jn. 1:14).
> Blackboard

I. SUBJECT MATTER
God Keeps His Promise
1. The Annunciation
2. The Visitation

II. TYPE
Development

III. OBJECTIVES
A. To develop a better understanding of the feasts of the Annunciation and Visitation.
B. To impress upon the children Mary's virtues of obedience, humility, and kindness.
C. To develop a greater love for Mary, the Mother of Jesus.
D. To increase the desire of imitating Mary's virtues, especially her obedience, humility, and kindness.

IV. MATERIALS
A. Pictures of the Annunciation and the Visitation.
B. Poem: "Hail, Full of Grace," Sister Josita Belger, *Sing a Song of Holy Things*, p. 55.

V. PROCEDURE

A. Approach
We have already learned how people prepared for the Saviour. Mary, too, was preparing for the Redeemer to come. However, God had something special to tell Mary about the Saviour.

B. Presentation
1. Explanation and discussion:
   a) Show picture and vividly tell the story of the Annunciation.
   b) Develop the heavenly conversation of the highest of angels with the sinless Mary.
   c) Discuss God's choice of a Mother for His Son, Jesus; stress especially her purity, piety, humility.
   d) Discuss Mary's husband, St. Joseph. (Explain role of foster father.)
   e) Explain and discuss Gabriel's message about Elizabeth; Mary's hastening to Elizabeth. Tell the story vividly, showing the picture.
   f) Explain and develop the words of greeting between Mary and Elizabeth.
   g) Explain how the Church remembers the words of Gabriel and Elizabeth in prayer "Hail Mary."
2. Application:
   a) Discuss ways in which we can honor Mary by imitating her virtues of kindness, obedience, and humility.
   b) Discuss ways in which we can show kindness at home and at school.
3. Organization:
   The children may have a dialog between Mary and Angel Gabriel, and Mary and Elizabeth, stressing their greetings.
4. Broader Appreciation:
   Poem: "Hail, Full of Grace," Sister Josita Belger, *Sing a Song of Holy Things*, p. 55.
5. Assignment:
   None
6. Suggested Activity:
   Make a class composition on how to show kindness at school.

UNIT THREE, PART 5 (cont.).

LESSON PLAN 66

Children read or reread and discuss Parts 4 and 5, pp. 104–112, in their text.

UNIT THREE, PART 5 (cont.).

LESSON PLAN 67

> "Blessed art thou, O Virgin Mary, by the Lord God most High, above all women upon the earth" (Raccolta, 311).
> Blackboard

I. SUBJECT MATTER
The prayer: "The Angelus"

II. TYPE
Development

III. MATERIALS
Prayer "The Angelus," p. 5, in children's text.

IV. PROCEDURE
See plan for "Act of Faith," Unit 2, Lesson 30, p. 26, in Manual.

UNIT THREE, PARTS 6 AND 7, LESSON PLANS 68–70, The Birth of Our Saviour.
The Shepherds at the Crib. Text, pp. 112, 115

LESSON PLAN 68

> "Glory to God in the highest; and on earth peace to men of good will" (Lk. 2:14).
> Blackboard

I. SUBJECT MATTER
The Birth of Our Saviour
The Shepherds at the Crib

II. TYPE
Development

III. OBJECTIVES
A. To develop a greater understanding of the events pertinent to the Nativity.
B. To develop an appreciation of God's goodness in sending us a Saviour.
C. To increase the desire of preparing oneself better for the coming of Jesus.

IV. MATERIALS
A. Pictures of the Nativity and adoration of the shepherds.
B. Poem: Christmas poems, Sister Josita Belger, *Sing a Song of Holy Things*, pp. 27, 35.

V. PROCEDURE

A. Approach
Recall briefly the message of the Angel Gabriel to Mary.

B. Presentation
1. Explanation and discussion:
   a) Tell the story of the Nativity vividly under the caption:
      1) Caesar's decree
      2) Mary and Joseph's journey to Bethlehem
      3) Finding of stable
      4) Nativity
      5) Angel's message to the shepherds
      6) Visit of shepherds
   b) Explain that the Infant born is Jesus Christ, the Son of God, the Second Person of the Blessed Trinity, true God and true Man.
   c) Develop "Adoration" through the actions of the shepherds.
   d) Develop "Glory to God" and "Peace to men of good will" through the actions of the angels.
   e) Explain that heaven (angels) and earth (shepherds) recognized Jesus as God by adoring Him.
2. Application:
   a) Let us visit Jesus, our God, in the church as the shepherds visited Him in the stable.
   b) Discuss ways in preparing our hearts for His coming.
   c) The children resolve to receive Jesus in Holy Communion often in preparation for Christmas.
3. Organization:
   The children dramatize scenes from the Christmas story.
4. Broader Appreciation:
   Choice of Christmas poems from *Sing a Song of Holy Things*, pp. 27–35.
5. Assignment:
   Catechism question 45, p. 132, at the end of Unit Three in children's text.
6. Suggested Activities:
   a) The children make a spiritual crib.
   b) The children recite choral Christmas poems to another class.

UNIT THREE, PARTS 6 AND 7 (cont.).

LESSON PLAN 69

> "O Jesus, the friend of little children, bless the little children of the whole world" (Raccolta, 78).
> Blackboard

I. SUBJECT MATTER
The True Meaning of Christmas

II. TYPE
Appreciation

III. OBJECTIVES
A. To appreciate the real meaning of Christmas as the birth of the Christ Child.
B. To develop gratitude and appreciation for the Christmas gift given us by God.
C. To instill in the children the attitude that giving is more important than receiving.

IV. MATERIALS
A. Pictures depicting enjoyable scenes of Christmas.
B. Poem: "Why I am Happy at Christmas," Sister Josita Belger, *Sing a Song of Holy Things*, p. 27.

V. PROCEDURE

A. Approach
Children express their ideas of what Christmas really means to them.

B. Presentation

1. Explanation and discussion:
   a) Explain and discuss how God made the first Christmas a Christmas of love — He gave us His Son Jesus to make us happy; discuss how He made it a feast of giving.
   b) Explain and discuss how Christmas can be a feast of love and happiness.
   c) Discuss the true meaning of Christmas — giving to make others happy.
   d) Discuss ways of showing the true meaning of Christmas.

2. Application:
Children decide how they will show a true Christmas spirit in their own homes.

3. Broader Appreciation:
Poem: "Why I Am Happy at Christmas," Sister Josita Belger, *Sing a Song of Holy Things*, p. 27.

4. Suggested Activities:
   a) Children learn and recite often the ejaculation: "O Jesus, the Friend of little children, etc." (*Raccolta*, 78)
   b) The children write a composition on the true meaning of Christmas.
   c) The children write letters to the Christ Child.

UNIT THREE, PARTS 6 AND 7 (cont.).

LESSON PLAN 70

Children read or reread and discuss Parts 6 and 7, pp. 112–117, in their text.

UNIT THREE, PART 8, LESSON PLANS 71–72, Jesus Is Presented in the Temple. Text, p. 117

LESSON PLAN 71

> "Now Thou dost dismiss Thy servant, O Lord, according to Thy word in peace" (Lk. 2:29).
> Blackboard

I. SUBJECT MATTER
Jesus is Presented in the Temple

II. TYPE
Development

III. OBJECTIVES
A. To develop an understanding of the Feast of the Presentation of Jesus.
B. To create the desire to please God always by obeying His commands.
C. To increase the desire of imitating Mary's purity and obedience.

IV. MATERIALS
Picture of the Presentation of Jesus.

V. PROCEDURE

A. Approach
Do you know the story of our Lord's first visit to the temple?

B. Presentation

1. Explanation and discussion:
   a) Tell vividly the story of the Presentation showing the picture; also offering of the doves and the words of Simeon and Anna.
   b) Discuss the sentiments of each person.
   c) Tell why Simeon called Jesus "The Light of the World."
   d) Explain and discuss how the Church celebrates this feast every year. (Candlemas)
   e) Explain and discuss the purpose of the blessed candles in church and at home.

2. Application:
Simeon was able to hold Jesus. How much more privileged are we to receive Jesus in Holy Communion. The children resolve to receive Jesus often.

3. Organization:
   a) Why was Jesus taken to the temple forty days after His birth?
   b) What offering did Mary make to God?
   c) What holy man was in the temple at that time?
   d) Why was he there?
   e) What did Simeon know when he saw Jesus?
   f) When Simeon had Jesus in his arms, what did he say to God?
   g) Of what did Simeon speak to Mary?

4. Broader Appreciation:
Explain and recite in simple language the "*Nunc Dimittis*" (Lk. 2:29–32).

5. Suggested Activity:
The children make up original prayers telling God they want to belong to Him.

UNIT THREE, PART 8 (cont.).

LESSON PLAN 72

The children read or reread and discuss Part 8, p. 117, in their text.

UNIT THREE, PART 9, LESSON PLANS 73–74, The Wise Men Worship the Saviour. Text, p. 120

LESSON PLAN 73

> "And entering into the house, they found the Child with Mary His Mother, and falling down they adored Him" (Mt. 2:11).
>
> Blackboard

I. SUBJECT MATTER
The Wise Men Worship the Saviour

II. TYPE
Development

III. OBJECTIVES
A. To appreciate God's great gift to us — His only Son.
B. To develop an attitude of love for and faith in Jesus and the desire to attend Mass regularly.
C. To increase the desire of making sacrifices for love of Jesus.

IV. MATERIALS
A. Picture of the Magi.
B. Poem: "The Wise Men," Sister Josita Belger, *Sing a Song of Holy Things*," pp. 38–39.

V. PROCEDURE

A. Approach
Discuss briefly visits from some special friend and gifts received.

B. Presentation
1. Explanation and discussion:
   a) Tell vividly the story of the Magi; show various pictures of Magi and discuss.
   b) Explain the purpose and meaning of their gifts:
   gold — Jesus is King; love
   incense — Jesus is God; prayer
   myrrh — Jesus is Man; sacrifice
   c) Compare the gifts of the Wise Men with the gifts we can offer to the Christ Child especially when preparing for Holy Communion:
   gold — our love
   incense — our fervent prayers
   myrrh — our little penances and sacrifices
   d) compare the star with our sanctuary lamp in church.
   e) Discuss the hardships endured during the long trip; compare it to our ease at attending church services out of love for Jesus.
2. Application:
   Let us make our gifts for Jesus consist of love, prayers, and sacrifices.
3. Organization:
   Children retell and discuss the story.
4. Broader Appreciation:
   Poem: "The Wise Men," Sister Josita Belger, *Sing a Song of Holy Things*, pp. 38–39.
5. Suggested Activity:
   The children draw pictures of the Magi.

UNIT THREE, PART 9 (cont.).

LESSON PLAN 74

The children read or reread and discuss Part 9, p. 120, in their text.

UNIT THREE, PART 10, LESSON PLANS 75–77. Life at Nazareth. Text, pp. 123–124

LESSON PLAN 75

> "Behold an angel appeared in sleep to Joseph saying: Arise, and take the child and his mother, and fly into Egypt" (Mt. 2:13).
>
> Blackboard

I. SUBJECT MATTER
The Flight Into Egypt

II. TYPE
Development

III. OBJECTIVES
A. To develop the knowledge of the hardships endured during the flight into Egypt.
B. To increase the desire to do always what God wants us to do.
C. To foster an attitude of obeying willingly and cheerfully.

IV. MATERIALS
Picture: Flight Into Egypt.

V. PROCEDURE

A. Approach
Recall the visit of the Magi and Herod's request.

B. Presentation
1. Explanation and discussion:
   a) Explain how Herod planned to kill Jesus, how Wise Men and St. Joseph were informed of his plan.
   b) Show picture and tell vividly the story of the Flight into Egypt.
   c) Stress the fact that Joseph's prompt obedience saved the life of the Infant Jesus.
   d) Tell vividly the story of the Holy Innocents and their eternal reward.

2. Application:
Try to do as asked even when it is difficult. Cite examples. Like the Holy Family, let us place our trust in God's loving care.
3. Organization:
The children retell the story of the Flight into Egypt in sequence.

UNIT THREE, PART 10 (cont.).

LESSON PLAN 76

> "But when Herod was dead behold an angel of the Lord appeared in sleep to Joseph" (Mt. 2:19).
> Blackboard

I. SUBJECT MATTER
Life at Nazareth

II. TYPE
Development

III. OBJECTIVES
A. To become acquainted with the life of the Holy Family at Nazareth.
B. To appreciate and encourage the practice of the virtues exemplified by the Holy Family.
C. To develop a greater appreciation of our own home life by trying to spread joy, happiness, and love.

IV. MATERIALS
A. Pictures depicting scenes of the Holy Family in Nazareth.
B. Poems: "Just Think," p. 49, and "Learning," p. 38, Thayer, *Child on His Knees*.

V. PROCEDURE

A. Approach
How long did the Holy Family remain in Egypt? The children give their ideas.

B. Presentation
1. Explanation and discussion:
   a) Explain and discuss the command of the angel to the Holy Family to return to Holy Land; explain reason for Holy Family's choice of Nazareth for their home; locate Nazareth on classroom map.
   b) Discuss family life at Nazareth and compare with our home conditions
      1) Type of home
      2) Work of each member of the Holy Family
      3) Food and clothing
      4) Entertainment
      5) Travel
      6) Prayers

   c) Explain that life at Nazareth was difficult, but the Holy Family was content and led a happy home life.
   d) Discuss the obedience of the Christ Child and the spirit of love and helpfulness which prevailed in the home.
2. Applications:
The children discuss their own home life comparing it with the life of the Holy Family.
The children suggest ways in which they can make their home one of love, helpfulness, prayer, and obedience.
3. Organization:
The children make a report of an imaginary trip to Nazareth.
4. Broader Appreciation:
Poems: "Just Think," and "Learning," Thayer, *Child on His Knees*, p. 38.
5. Suggested Activity:
The children write a prayer to Jesus, asking Him to make their home life as happy as His was.

UNIT THREE, PART 10 (cont.).

LESSON PLAN 77

The children read or reread and discuss Part 10, p. 123, in their text.

UNIT THREE, PART 11, LESSON PLANS 78, 79, The Child Jesus in the Temple. Text, p. 125

LESSON PLAN 78

> "And He went down with them and came to Nazareth and was subject to them" (Lk. 2:5).
> Blackboard

I. SUBJECT MATTER
The Child Jesus in the Temple

II. TYPE
Development

III. OBJECTIVES
A. To develop an understanding of the purpose of the visit to the temple.
B. To develop an appreciation of the privilege we have of attending Sunday and daily Mass; also of saying prayers to Jesus in the Blessed Sacrament.
C. To develop an attitude of reverence and respect in church.

IV. MATERIALS
A. Picture: Jesus Teaching in the Temple. Hymn: The Joyful Mysteries, *People's Hymnal*, No. R-15.

V. PROCEDURE

A. Approach

Recall the happy home life of the Holy Family. Bring out the fact that Jesus was now privileged to go where He hadn't gone before.

B. Presentation

1. Explanation and discussion:
    a) Explain the custom of celebrating the Feast of the Passover in Jerusalem, and the Holy Family's attendance in obedience to the law.
    b) Tell vividly the story of the loss and finding of Jesus; show picture and discuss.
    c) Discuss the Holy Family's reverence at prayer; compare it to our reverence in church.
    d) Discuss our privilege of having a church so close that we can visit it daily.
    e) Discuss the prompt obedience of Jesus; compare it to our obedience.
2. Application:
    The children resolve to obey their parents and teachers cheerfully and promptly as Jesus did. The children try to imitate Jesus at prayer by praying well at all times.
3. Organization:
    Children retell the story.
4. Broader Appreciation:
    Hymn: The Joyful Mysteries, *People's Hymnal*, No. R-15.
5. Suggested Activity:
    The children bring to school pictures depicting someone at prayer or going to Mass. Discuss them.

UNIT THREE, PART 11 (cont.).

LESSON PLAN 79

The children read or reread and discuss Part 11, p. 125, in their text.

UNIT THREE, PART 12, LESSON PLANS 80–83, Jesus Is God Made Man. Text, p. 128.

LESSON PLAN 80

> "And the Child grew and was strong, full of wisdom; and the grace of God was in Him" (Lk. 2:40).
>
> Blackboard

I. SUBJECT MATTER

Jesus Is God Made Man

II. TYPE

Development

III. OBJECTIVES

A. To develop the knowledge that Jesus is both God and Man.
B. To develop the knowledge that Jesus has a human nature and a divine nature.
C. To develop an attitude of greater love for Jesus who came down to earth because He loved us.

IV. MATERIALS

Picture of the Christ Child.

V. PROCEDURE

A. Approach

When you look into the crib or at these pictures whom do you see?

B. Presentation

1. Explanation and discussion:
    a) Explain that the Infant is Jesus Christ, the Son of God, the second Person of the Blessed Trinity, true God and true Man.
    b) The little hands, feet, face (human form) say that He is man; the halo above His head is a way of saying that He is God.
    c) Explain what we mean when we say that Jesus is God-made-Man.
    d) Explain and discuss our human nature:
        1) We are one person.
        2) We have one nature (human nature).
        3) Our nature has a body and a soul.
        4) We can act and think as a human being.
    e) Explain Jesus' nature — two natures, human and divine.
        1) Jesus has divine nature because:
            (a) Jesus is God.
            (b) Jesus can work miracles.
            (c) He can do what God can do.
        2) Jesus has also a human nature because:
            (a) Jesus is man (He has a body and a soul).
            (b) He can act and think as we do.
    f) Explain that Jesus has two natures but is One Person — a Divine Person.
    g) Explain and discuss ways in which Jesus showed both these natures in His life.
    h) End the presentation by repeating exact answers of the Revised Baltimore Catechism No. 1 (Confraternity), questions 41–45, Text, p. 132.
2. Application:
    The children resolve to love and imitate Jesus more because He took upon Himself a human nature to become a child like us.
3. Organization:
    a) Who is Jesus Christ?
    b) Is Jesus like us?
    c) In what way does Jesus resemble us?
    d) How many natures has Jesus?
    e) As God, what nature does Jesus have?

f) As man, what nature does Jesus have?

g) What can Jesus do because of His divine nature?

h) What can Jesus do because of His human nature?

4. Assignment:
Questions 41, 42, 43, 44, and 45, p. 132, at the end of Unit Three in children's text.

5. Broader Appreciation:
The children make up a prayer to thank Jesus for becoming man.

6. Suggested Activity:
The children find pictures in which Jesus portrays human and divine natures.

UNIT THREE, PART 12 (cont.).

LESSON PLAN 81

The children read or reread and discuss Part 12, p. 128, in their text.

UNIT THREE, PART 12 (cont.).

LESSON PLAN 82

I. SUBJECT MATTER
"Problems" at end of Unit Three, Part 12, p. 131.

II. TYPE
Discussion

III. MATERIALS
Same as for discussion plan Unit One, Lesson 8, in the Manual.

UNIT THREE, PART 12 (cont.).

LESSON PLAN 83

I. SUBJECT MATTER
God the Son Became Man

II. TYPE
Drill

III. MATERIALS
Questions at the end of Unit Three, p. 133, in the children's text.

IV. PROCEDURE
Same as for drill lesson, Unit One, Lesson 21, p. 18, in the Manual.

III. Culmination of Unit Three

LESSON PLAN 84

I. SUBJECT MATTER
God the Son Became Man

II. TYPE
Culmination

III. MATERIALS
A. Hymns, poems, stories, etc., developed during the Unit.

IV. PROCEDURE
Same as for culmination plan, Unit One, Lesson 22, p. 42, in the Manual.

IV. Evaluation of Unit Three

LESSON PLAN 85

The children take the written test found in their text at end of Unit Three, pp. 134–136.
After each Unit, reteach and retest where there are weaknesses revealed.

SPECIAL LESSONS FOR THE LITURGICAL YEAR (Unit Three)

December 8 — Immaculate Conception
"O Mary conceived without sin, pray for us who have recourse to thee." (*Raccolta*, 357)

December 25 — Nativity of Our Lord
"Blessed be Jesus Christ and His most pure Mother." (*Raccolta*, 80)

December 28 — The Holy Innocents
"My Jesus mercy." (*Raccolta*, 70)

January 1 — New Year
Sunday after New Year — Holy Name of Jesus
"Blessed be the Name of Jesus." (Divine Praises)

January 6 — Epiphany
"Jesus, Mary, Joseph." (*Raccolta*, 274)

Sunday After Epiphany — The Holy Family
"Jesus, Mary, and Joseph, I give you my heart and my soul." (*Raccolta*, 636)

CORRELATED ACTIVITIES FOR UNIT THREE

Art

1. The children make a frieze illustrating the Christmas story.
2. The children make a picture book showing kind

children getting ready for the birthday of the Christ Child.
3. The children draw pictures illustrating any stories learned during this Unit.
4. The children have a "Treasure Hunt" to find as many pictures as possible depicting the stories learned during this Unit. They arrange them in a scrapbook, or on the bulletin board with the proper captions.
5. Picture study: "The Return From Egypt."
6. Make symbols for "Jesus," "Christ," "Mary."

English

1. The children compose poems, stories, or sentences about facts taught in this Unit.
2. The children dramatize the entire Christmas story.
3. The children memorize poems taken during this Unit.
4. The children write letters to someone sick, hoping to make him happy during the Christmas season.
5. The children play a "Who" game, using characters from this Unit and asking "Who" questions about them.
6. The children play a "Make Believe" game. They pretend they are one of the characters of this Unit, and tell one thing that they did.

Music

1. Use as many appropriate Christmas hymns as possible. Imbue the children with the understanding that Christmas is Christ's birthday — Jesus became Man.
2. Hymns:
   a) "Joyful Mysteries of the Rosary," *The People's Hymnal*, pp. 86 and 87, No. R-15.
   b) "O Come, O Come Emmanuel," *The People's Hymnal*, p. 15, No. A-1.
   c) "Creator of the Stars of Night," *The People's Hymnal*, No. A-5.

Science

1. The children plan a science unit on stars.

UNIT FOUR. *JESUS DIES FOR US*

(Text, *God's Truths Help Us Live,* pp. 137–176)

(Revised Baltimore Catechism No. 1 [Confraternity], Questions 40–45.)

INTRODUCTORY MATERIAL

I. INTRODUCTION FOR THE TEACHER

This Unit considers the accomplishment of our Redemption by Christ. It begins with the public ministry of Christ and continues with His Passion and death on the cross, His Resurrection and Ascension. A section of this Unit is devoted to the Sacrifice of the Mass, developing more fully the three principal parts.

II. OBJECTIVES OF THE UNIT

A. To gain a greater understanding of God's great and fatherly love in sending us the Redeemer.
B. To cultivate a deep feeling of gratitude to Jesus in return for His great love for us.
C. To strive to imitate the virtues of Jesus, especially His obedience, courage, kindness, and love of prayer.
D. To learn to assist at Mass properly, with fitting attention and devotion.

III. SUBJECT MATTER

A. The Redeemer begins His Public Life and Work
  1. The Baptism of Jesus
  2. The Temptation in the Desert
  3. Choosing of the Apostles
  4. Some Miracles of Jesus
B. Jesus offered Himself on the cross as the true Sacrifice of the New Law
  1. How Jesus offered Himself (Passion)
  2. Why Jesus offered Himself
C. Jesus offers Himself in the Mass today
  1. How Jesus offers Himself
  2. Why Jesus offers Himself in the Mass
  3. What we do at Holy Mass
D. Jesus prepared a place for us
  1. Jesus rose from the dead
  2. Jesus ascended into heaven
  3. Jesus will come to judge the world

IV. TEACHER REFERENCES FOR UNIT FOUR

1. Baierl, Rev. Joseph, *The Creed Explained,* pp. 290–358.
2. Belger, Sister Mary Josita, C.S.F., *Sing a Song of Holy Things,* 56–57, 58–59, 75–79, 84–85.
3. Johnson, George, *The Bible Story,* pp. 162–225.
4. Lovasik, Lawrence G., *Catechism Sketched,* pp. 25–27.
5. Montani, *St. Gregory Hymnal,* pp. 134, 239.
6. *People's Hymnal,* No. R-8, R-16, R-17.
7. Thayer, Mary Dixon, *The Child on His Knees,* pp. 52–53, 75, 81, 101.

LESSON PLANS FOR UNIT FOUR

I. Introduction to Unit Four

Jesus Dies for Us. Text, p. 137

LESSON PLAN 86

I. SUBJECT MATTER
Jesus Dies for Us

II. TYPE
Introduction

III. MATERIALS
Unit Four, p. 137 in children's text.

IV. PROCEDURE
Same as for introductory lesson for Unit Two, Lesson 1, in Manual.

II. Work Study Periods for Unit Four
(Lesson Plans 87–112)

UNIT FOUR, PART 1, Jesus Begins His Public Life. Text, p. 138

LESSON PLAN 87

> "This is My beloved Son, in whom I am well pleased" (Mt. 3:17).
> Blackboard

I. SUBJECT MATTER
Jesus Begins His Public Life and Work
The Baptism of Jesus

II. TYPE
Development

III. OBJECTIVES
A. To develop the knowledge of how Jesus began His public ministry and of the manifestation of the Blessed Trinity at that time.
B. To incite the children to recite the "Glory be to the Father" with greater attention and understanding.
C. To instill in the children love for the Blessed Trinity.

IV. MATERIALS
The Bible Story, Johnson, pp. 162-165.

V. PROCEDURE

A. Approach
Discuss with the children the length of time our Lord spent at Nazareth. Discuss: Did people know he was God?

B. Presentation
1. Explanation and discussion:
   a) Contrast the hidden life of Jesus at Nazareth with the life He would now live; mention the hardships connected with such a life — lack of shelter, constant travel, irregular meals, etc.
   b) Tell purpose of this life — to prove that He is God, and redeem the world.
   c) Read the story of the baptism of Jesus from the Bible or tell the story vividly; show how our Lord's baptism was a manifestation of the Blessed Trinity; discuss reason for the baptism of Jesus.
2. Application:
   Children resolve to lead lives worthy of God's praise — "This is my beloved Son in whom I am well pleased."
3. Organization:
   a) How old was Jesus when He started His public life?
   b) What was the public life of Jesus?
   c) Why was Jesus baptized?
   d) Why did John hesitate to baptize Jesus?
   e) What mystery was shown to the people on the day that Jesus was baptized?
4. Broader Appreciation:
   a) Story — "John Baptizes Jesus," Johnson, *The Bible Story*, pp. 162-165.
   b) Have children learn ejaculation, "Thou art Christ, the Son of the living God."
5. Assignment:
   None
6. Suggested Activity:
   Pupils learn to chant *"Gloria Patri."*

UNIT FOUR, PART 1 (cont.).

LESSON PLAN 88

Children read or reread and discuss Part 1, p. 138, in their text.

UNIT FOUR, PART 2, LESSON PLANS 89-90, Jesus Is Tempted by the Devil. Text, p. 141

LESSON PLAN 89

> "The Lord thy God shalt thou worship and Him only shalt thou serve" (Mt. 4:10).
> Blackboard

I. SUBJECT MATTER
Jesus is Tempted by the Devil

II. TYPE
Development

III. OBJECTIVES
A. To develop the story of Christ's temptation and the reason for it.
B. To arouse the children to spurn the devil in time of temptation, as Jesus did.
C. To bring about in the children an appreciation of God's help in time of temptation.

IV. MATERIALS
The Bible Story, Johnson, pp. 165-166.

V. PROCEDURE

A. Approach
What did Jesus do right after His baptism? (Discuss)

B. Presentation
1. Explanation and discussion:
   a) Tell vividly the story of Christ's forty days' fast in the desert and His temptation by the devil.
   b) Discuss reasons for our Lord's temptation:
      1) Devil wanted to find out if Jesus was God.
      2) Jesus wanted to show us that we too must expect temptation.
   c) Discuss the manner of Christ's dealing with the devil.
   d) Discuss temptations in our lives: what they are, when they become sinful, how we should deal with them; show how we should deal with them; show how we can sometimes avoid them.
2. Application:
   Pupils resolve to use short ejaculations upon awareness of a temptation.

3. Organization:
List with the children the tempting words of the devil and our Lord's answer each time.
4. Broader Appreciation:
   a) Story: "Jesus Is Tempted by the Devil," Johnson, *The Bible Story*, pp. 165–166.
   b) Children compose ejaculatory prayers for use in time of temptations.
5. Suggested Activity:
Pupils may write the short prayers just composed and paste them in a class prayer book. Illustrate book with holy pictures.

UNIT FOUR, PART 2 (cont.).

LESSON PLAN 90

Children read or reread and discuss Part 2, p. 141, in their text.

UNIT FOUR, PART 3, LESSON PLANS 91–92, Jesus Chooses His Apostles. Text, p. 143

LESSON PLAN 91

> "You have not chosen Me; I have chosen you" (Jn. 15:16)
>
> Blackboard

I. SUBJECT MATTER
Jesus Chooses His Apostles

II. TYPE
Development

III. OBJECTIVES
A. To gain an understanding of how our Lord went about beginning the work of His Redemption.
B. To cultivate a deep love for Jesus.
C. To strive to become worthy of His special attention and love.

IV. MATERIALS
The Bible Story, Johnson, pp. 166–169.

V. PROCEDURE

A. Approach
What was the biggest thing Jesus was to do during His public life? (Die for our sins)

B. Presentation
1. Explanation and discussion:
   a) Explain why Jesus founded His Church as a way to continue the work of redemption; explain that this Church would last till the end of the world so Jesus needed helpers to spread His kingdom here on earth.
   b) Tell how Jesus chose these helpers. Have pupils study the names of the Apostles. Discuss: "What kind of helpers did Jesus want?" Explain how the Apostles would learn much from Jesus by staying with Him every day.
   c) Discuss: Help the Apostles would give Jesus during and after His Public Life.
2. Application:
How can we be helpers of Jesus in spreading His kingdom all over the world? Children resolve to help others know about the Church.
3. Organization:
   a) Who were the Apostles?
   b) Why were they chosen?
   c) What kind of men were they?
4. Broader Appreciation:
Story: "The First Disciples," Johnson, *The Bible Story*, pp. 166–169.

UNIT FOUR, PART 3 (cont.).

LESSON PLAN 92

Children read or reread and discuss Part 3, p. 143, in their text.

UNIT FOUR, PARTS 4, 5, LESSON PLANS 93–95. Text, pp. 145–150.

LESSON PLAN 93

> "By their fruits you shall know them" (Mt. 7:20).
>
> Blackboard

I. SUBJECT MATTER
The Miracles of Jesus

II. TYPE
Development

III. OBJECTIVES
A. To develop the knowledge of how Jesus Christ proved that He is God through His miracles.
B. To arouse a deep reverence for Jesus as God.
C. To strive to imitate the love and kindness of Jesus.

IV. MATERIALS
Pictures depicting some miracles of Jesus.
Poem: "To the Blessed Mother," Thayer, *Child on His Knees*, p. 81.

V. PROCEDURE

A. Approach
What are some of the things that Jesus did during His last three years on earth?

B. Presentation
1. Explanation and discussion:
   a) Discuss and explain the meaning of the word: miracle.
   b) Explain how Jesus drew the people to love and believe in Him because of the miracles He performed.
   c) Mention and discuss the following miracles with children:
      1) Marriage Feast of Cana (Text, p. 145).
      2) Multiplication of Loaves (Text, p. 148).
   d) Children discuss other miracles of Jesus which they have heard.
2. Application:
   Children resolve to increase their love for God after hearing about His power and goodness to men.
3. Broader Appreciation:
   Poem: "To the Blessed Mother."
4. Suggested Activity:
   Children draw or collect pictures of the miracles of Jesus and make booklets.

UNIT FOUR, PARTS 4 AND 5 (cont.).

LESSON PLAN 94

> "Behold the Lamb of God, Who takes away the sin of the world" (Jn. 1:29).
> Blackboard

I. SUBJECT MATTER
Jesus Begins His Public Life

II. TYPE
Discussion

III. PROCEDURE
Same as for discussion plan, Unit One, Lesson 8, in Manual.

UNIT FOUR, PARTS 4 AND 5 (cont.).

LESSON PLAN 95

Children read or reread and discuss Parts 4 and 5, pp. 145–150, in their text.

UNIT FOUR, PART 6, LESSON PLAN 96, Palm Sunday. Text, p. 150

LESSON PLAN 96

> "Blessed is He that cometh in the name of the Lord: Hosanna in the Highest" (Raccolta, 139).
> Blackboard

I. SUBJECT MATTER
Palm Sunday

II. TYPE
Development

III. OBJECTIVES
A. To relate the story of our Lord's coming into Jerusalem.
B. To give a realization of the value and meaning of blessed palms.
C. To arouse a deep love for Jesus who is beginning His great sacrifice.

IV. MATERIALS
Picture of Jesus entering Jerusalem.

V. PROCEDURE

A. Approach
Discuss with the children the chief purpose of our Lord's coming to this world.

B. Presentation
1. Explanation and discussion:
   a) Explain that the time had now come for our Lord to offer Himself as a sacrifice of the New Law.
   b) Tell that Jesus Christ began His actual sacrifice or Passion by His entry into Jerusalem.
   c) Show picture and tell vividly the story of our Lord's entry in Jerusalem; explain that there were friends and enemies in the crowd that met Him.
   d) Discuss the present-day manner in which the Catholic Church celebrates this event.
   e) Explain the use of blessed palms, manner of destroying them, and what happens to the blessed palms after the feast (used for Ash Wednesday).
2. Application:
   Children resolve to attend the Mass (if possible) during which the palms are blessed.
3. Organization:
   Have pupils retell the story of our Lord's entry into Jerusalem.
4. Broader Appreciation and Suggested Activity:
   Have pupils collect palms and make crosses.

UNIT FOUR, PART 6 (cont.).

LESSON PLAN 97

Children read or reread and discuss Part 6, p. 150, in their text.

UNIT FOUR, PART 7, LESSON PLANS 98, 99, Holy Thursday. Text, p. 153

LESSON PLAN 98

> "This is My Body" (Mt. 26:26).
> Blackboard

I. **SUBJECT MATTER**
Holy Thursday

II. **TYPE**
Development

III. **OBJECTIVES**
 A. To develop the knowledge of how our Lord offered Himself as the Sacrifice of the New Law.
 B. To incite the children to receive the sacrament of the Holy Eucharist often.
 C. To instill in the children gratitude to our Lord in the Holy Eucharist.

IV. **MATERIALS**
Picture of the Last Supper.

V. **PROCEDURE**

 A. Approach
 Discuss: What great and wonderful thing did Jesus do on the day before He died?

 B. Presentation
 1. Explanation and discussion:
  a) Relate as graphically as possible the story of the Last Supper; show picture and discuss.
   1) Stress the fact that our Lord instituted the Holy Eucharist in order to remain with us, out of love.
   2) Bring out main events that took place during the Last Supper:
    (a) Institution of the sacrament of the Holy Eucharist.
    (b) Institution of the sacrament of Holy Orders.
    (c) Celebration of the First Mass.
   3) Speak of our Lord's sadness during the Last Supper.
   4) Recall how the Catholic Church keeps this feast each year.
  b) Relate happenings of the same evening.
   1) Agony in Garden
   2) Betrayal
   3) Trials
   4) Peter's denial
   5) Imprisonment
 2. Application:
 Children resolve to show their love and gratitude to Jesus by receiving Him often in the sacrament of the Holy Eucharist.

 3. Organization:
 List on board the events of Holy Thursday in sequence.
 4. Broader Appreciation:
 Picture study of the Last Supper.
 5. Suggested Activity:
 Children write a three-sentence story about the Last Supper.

UNIT FOUR, PART 7 (cont.).

LESSON PLAN 99

Children read or reread and discuss Part 7, p. 153, in their text.

UNIT FOUR, PART 8, LESSON PLANS 100–102, Jesus Offers Himself for Us on the Cross — Good Friday. Text, p. 155

LESSON PLAN 100

> "We adore Thee, O Christ, and we bless Thee; because by Thy Cross Thou hast redeemed the world" (Raccolta, 197).
> Blackboard

I. **SUBJECT MATTER**
Good Friday

II. **TYPE**
Development

III. **OBJECTIVES**
 A. To relate the story of the crucifixion and burial of Jesus.
 B. To arouse in the children sorrow for sin.
 C. To instill in the children a desire to better their acts.

IV. **MATERIALS**
"Thirteenth Station," Sister Josita Belger, *Sing a Song of Holy Things*, p. 75.

V. **PROCEDURE**

 A. Approach
 Recall briefly the principal events of Holy Week that took place thus far.

 B. Presentation
 1. Explanation and discussion:
  a) Relate the events of Good Friday, beginning with the unfair trial by Pilate, the unjust scourging and crowning with thorns. Our Lord's bravery in it all.

- *b)* Describe the sad and painful journey to Calvary.
- *c)* Tell vividly about the crucifixion, stressing the stripping of garments, the nailing, and the erection of the cross.
- *d)* Discuss and explain the last words of Jesus on the cross.
- *e)* Tell of His last gift to us — His Mother.
- *f)* Speak of the death of Jesus on the cross, the reaction of the people and that of nature itself.
- *g)* Tell of the burial of Jesus, explain the term, Limbo, and what happened to the soul of Jesus at His death.
- *h)* Explain the symbols of the crucifixion.
- *i)* Discuss purpose of stations of the cross in the church.
- *j)* Teach the children a simple method of making the stations.
- *k)* End the presentation by repeating exact answers of the Revised Baltimore Catechism No. 1 (Confraternity) questions 46, 47, 48, Text, p. 172.

2. Application:
Remember how bravely our Lord Jesus Christ suffered for us. Resolve to be brave in avoiding all occasion of sin today.

3. Organization:
- *a)* What happened to us because of Adam's sin?
- *b)* What happened to us because of Jesus' death on the cross?
- *c)* What is Limbo?
- *d)* What happened to the soul of Jesus after His death?

4. Broader Appreciation:
Poem: "Thirteenth Station," Sister Josita Belger, *Sing a Song of Holy Things*, p. 75.

5. Assignment:
Catechism questions 46, 47, 48, p. 172, at end of Unit Four, in children's text.

6. Suggested Activity:
- *a)* Children write as nicely as possible the above prayer.
- *b)* Children draw symbols of the Passion.
- *c)* Children draw three black crosses and place on a violet background (very effective).

UNIT FOUR, PART 8 (cont.).

LESSON PLAN 101

> "Christ Jesus, my Helper and my Redeemer" (Raccolta, 85).
>
> **Blackboard**

I. SUBJECT MATTER
Jesus Offered Himself

II. TYPE
Development

III. OBJECTIVES
A. To develop the knowledge of the fourfold purpose of the Sacrifice of the New Law.
B. To arouse a heartfelt gratitude to our Lord for undergoing His Passion for us.
C. To instill in the children a desire to use the Sacrifice of the Mass for the same fourfold purpose.

IV. MATERIALS
"So Much," Thayer, *Child on His Knees*, p. 101.

V. PROCEDURE

A. Approach
Recall and discuss briefly the sufferings and death of our Lord. Ask — Why did Jesus suffer and die?

B. Presentation
1. Explanation and discussion.
   - *a)* Explain that the enormity of sin and the majesty of the One offended require divine retribution. Our Lord Jesus Christ was the only One who could do it and did so because of His great love for us; His great courage.
   - *b)* Explain the term: Redemption.
   - *c)* Recall sacrifices of the Old Law and compare them to the offering of self made by Jesus; explain that Jesus would be the only victim offered in sacrifice from now on. This sacrifice, called sacrifice of the New Law, is the Mass.
   - *d)* Explain that Jesus Christ offered Himself to God for the four reasons for which all sacrifice is offered.
      1) To adore God for us.
      2) To thank God for His favors.
      3) To make up for our sins.
      4) To ask God's blessings for all men.
   - *e)* Explain that Jesus suffered more than was necessary because of His great love for us.
   - *f)* Tell why Catholics do not eat meat on Friday.
   - *g)* Explain that through the sin of Adam heaven was closed, grace was lost. Through the death of Jesus, heaven was opened, grace was regained.
   - *h)* Discuss: what can we learn from the sufferings and death of Jesus? (love of God and evil of sin)

2. Application:
Children resolve to make little sacrifices to make up for sins.

3. Organization:
List the four reasons why sacrifice is offered.

4. Broader Appreciation:
Poem. "So Much," Thayer. *Child on His Knees*. p. 101.

5. Assignment:
   None
6. Suggested Activity:
   Have children memorize the poem, "So Much."

UNIT FOUR, PART 8 (cont.).

LESSON PLAN 102

> "My God I believe in Thee, I hope in Thee, I love Thee" (Raccolta, 37).
> Blackboard

I. SUBJECT MATTER
Act of Hope

II. TYPE
Development

III. PROCEDURE
See procedure for developing new prayer, Unit Two, Lesson 7, in Manual.

UNIT FOUR, PART 8 (cont.).

LESSON PLAN 103

The children read or reread and discuss Part 8, p. 155, in their text.

UNIT FOUR, PART 9, LESSON PLANS 104–106, Jesus Offers Himself in the Mass. Text, p. 161

LESSON PLAN 104

> "He was offered because it was His own will and He opened not His mouth" (Isa. 55:72).
> Blackboard

I. SUBJECT MATTER
How Jesus Offers Himself Today: The Mass

II. TYPE
Development

III. OBJECTIVES
A. To gain an understanding of how Jesus offers Himself today.
B. To cultivate a deep feeling of gratitude to Jesus in return for His great love for us.
C. To excite in the children a deeper devotion at Mass.

IV. MATERIALS
Pictures of the Mass or film strip on the Mass.

V. PROCEDURE
A. Approach
Discuss with the children the great sacrifice of Jesus. Ask: How does Jesus offer Himself today?

B. Presentation
1. Explanation and discussion:
   a) Recall the great sacrifice Jesus made of Himself on the cross.
   b) Discuss meaning of the word, sacrifice; recall why death on the cross was a real sacrifice.
   c) Discuss purpose and necessity of a sacrifice today.
   d) Explain that Jesus continues His sacrifice in the Mass. Explain that the priest is taking the place of Jesus.
   e) Explain why the sacrifice on the cross and the sacrifice of the Mass are the same; Priest and Victim are same — Jesus; explain how cross was bloody sacrifice, Mass is unbloody sacrifice.
   f) Explain that the Mass is divided into three principal parts:
      1) Offertory
      2) Consecration
      3) Communion
      Give a short explanation of each part, what Jesus does, what priest does, what we do.
2. Application:
   Children resolve to offer themselves with Jesus to God during the sacrifice of the Mass.
3. Organization:
   a) What are the main parts of the Mass?
   b) What happens during the Offertory of the Mass?
   c) What should we do during the Offertory? (Offer ourselves.)
   d) What takes place during the Consecration?
   e) What is the third important part of the Mass?
4. Broader Appreciation:
   Children study pictures of the principal parts of the Mass.
5. Suggested Activity:
   Children visit the sacristy and examine the vestments and all other articles used during the Mass.

UNIT FOUR, PART 9 (cont.).

LESSON PLAN 105

> "My Lord and my God" (Raccolta, 133).
> Blackboard

I. SUBJECT MATTER
How to Assist at Mass

II. TYPE
Development

III. OBJECTIVES
 A. To explain the principal parts of the Mass.
 B. To arouse in the children an appreciation of the Holy Sacrifice of the Mass.
 C. To incite in the children a desire to attend Mass frequently, with attention and devotion.

IV. MATERIALS

Mass Charts. Poem: "How Kind," Thayer, *Child on His Knees*, p. 75.

V. PROCEDURE

A. Approach

Discuss the four reasons Jesus had in offering Himself to God in the Sacrifice of the Cross. Compare with the reasons why the Sacrifice of the Mass is offered.

B. Presentation
1. Explanation and discussion:
   a) Discuss vessels, vestments, and other articles seen before and at Mass.
   b) Discuss the reasons for the priest's wearing of different colors at Mass.
   c) Explain simply, using charts, the ceremony of Holy Mass, what the priest does, what we do.
   d) Tell of the best way of assisting at Mass — offering it with Christ and receiving Holy Communion.
   e) Discuss the reverence we should have for a priest, since he is another Christ.
2. Application:
   Children resolve to follow the Mass with attention and love.
3. Organization:
   The children practice their actions at Mass.
4. Broader Appreciation:
   Poem: "How Kind," Thayer, *Child on His Knees*, p. 75.
5. Suggested Activity:
   Children construct an altar.

UNIT FOUR, PART 9 (cont.).

LESSON PLAN 106

Children read or reread and discuss Part 9, p. 161, in their text.

UNIT FOUR, PART 10, LESSON PLANS 107–108, Jesus Rises From the Dead. Text, p. 164

LESSON PLAN 107

> "Peace be to you! It is I, fear not" (Lk. 24:36).
> Blackboard

I. SUBJECT MATTER
The Resurrection

II. TYPE
Development

III. OBJECTIVES
 A. To develop the knowledge of the Resurrection story.
 B. To arouse a deep love for the risen Lord.
 C. To incite in the children the desire to some day rise in glory with our Lord.

IV. MATERIALS

Picture of the Resurrection.
Easter Poems, Sister Josita Belger, *Sing a Song of Holy Things*, pp. 75–79.

V. PROCEDURE

A. Approach

What was done with Jesus' body after He died on the cross? What happened to His soul?

B. Presentation
1. Explanation and discussion:
   a) Tell vividly the story of the Resurrection. Show picture and discuss.
   b) Explain and discuss the reasons for the Resurrection of Christ:
      1) To prove that He is God and overcame sin and Satan.
      2) To show us that we, too, will rise from the dead.
   c) Relate the several apparitions of Jesus on Easter Sunday.
   d) Describe the glorified body of Jesus.
   e) Explain that our bodies will also be glorified on the Last Day.
   f) End the presentation by repeating exact answer of the Revised Baltimore Catechism, No. 1 (Confraternity), question 49, Text, p. 173.
2. Application:
   The children resolve to lead a good life so they can enjoy the glory of Jesus on the Last Day.
3. Organization:
   The children dramatize the story of the Resurrection.
4. Broader Appreciation:
   Easter Poems.
5. Assignment: Catechism question 49, p. 173, at end of Unit Four in children's text.
6. Suggested Activity:
   The children make posters depicting the Easter story.

UNIT FOUR, PART 10 (cont.).

LESSON PLAN 108

Children read or reread and discuss Part 10. p. 164, in their text.

UNIT FOUR, PART 11, LESSON PLANS 109–112.

LESSON PLAN 109

> "I will see you again and your heart shall rejoice and your joy no one shall take from you" (Jn. 16:23).
>
> Blackboard

I. **SUBJECT MATTER**
  Jesus Ascends into Heaven

II. **TYPE**
  Development

III. **OBJECTIVES**
  A. To develop the knowledge of the Ascension of our Lord.
  B. To lead the children to show appreciation to Jesus for His great love for us.
  C. To instill in the children a desire to lead a good life in preparation for eternal life.

IV. **MATERIALS**
  "The Ascension," Sister Josita Belger, *Sing a Song of Holy Things*, pp. 84 and 85.

V. **PROCEDURE**
  Picture the Ascension.

  A. **Approach**
    "How long did Jesus stay on earth after His Resurrection?"

  B. **Presentation**
  1. Explanation and discussion:
    a) Discuss the work of Jesus during the forty days after His Resurrection.
    b) Show picture and tell vividly the story of the Ascension.
      1) Mention the command Jesus gave to the Apostles before leaving them.
      2) Mention ways in which this command was carried out.
    c) Explain why Jesus went back to heaven:
      1) His work on earth was finished.
      2) He wanted to enter into His Kingdom.
      3) He wanted to send down the Holy Spirit.
      4) He wanted to pray to His Father for us.
      5) He wanted to prepare a place for us.
    d) Discuss: what place did Jesus get in heaven? Explain term: right hand of God. Will He ever leave that place? (Refer briefly to second coming of Christ.)
    e) End the presentation by repeating exact answer to the Revised Baltimore Catechism No. 1 (Confraternity) questions 50, 51, 52, Text, p. 173.

  2. Application:
    Children resolve to prepare for heaven every day just as Jesus did.
  3. Organization:
    List on board the reasons for the Ascension.
  4. Broader Appreciation: Poem: "The Ascension," Sister Josita Belger, *Sing a Song of Holy Things*, pp. 84, 85.
  5. Assignment:
    Catechism questions 50, 51, 52, p. 173, at end of Unit Four in children's text.
  6. Suggested Activity:
    Children make a sand-table layout on the Ascension showing Mount Olivet and the surrounding places.

LESSON PLAN 110

The children read or reread and discuss Unit Four, Part 11, p. 167, in their text.

LESSON PLAN 111

I. **SUBJECT MATTER**
  "Problems"

II. **TYPE**
  Discussion

III. **MATERIALS**
  Children's text, at the end of Unit Four, pp. 170–172.

IV. **PROCEDURE**
  Same as for discussion plan found for Unit One, Lesson 8, p. 13, in Manual.

LESSON PLAN 112

I. **SUBJECT MATTER**
  The Redemption

II. **TYPE**
  Drill

III. **MATERIALS**
  Questions at end of Unit Four, pp. 173–174, in children's text.

IV. **PROCEDURE**
  Same as for drill lesson, Unit One, Lesson 21, p. 41, in Manual.

III. Culmination of Unit Four

LESSON PLAN 113

I. **SUBJECT MATTER**
  Jesus Dies for Us

II. TYPE
Culmination

III. MATERIALS
Hymns, poems, stories, etc., developed during this Unit.

IV. PROCEDURE
Same as for culmination plan, Unit One, Lesson 22, p. 19, in Manual.

IV. Evaluation of Unit Four

LESSON PLAN 114

The children take the written test, pp. 175–176, found at the end of Unit Four in their Text. Reteach and retest as required.

SPECIAL LESSONS FOR THE LITURGICAL YEAR (Unit Four)

January 21 — St. Agnes
Prayer: "St. Agnes, virgin and martyr, pray for us."

February 2 — The Purification
Prayer: "And thy own soul a sword shall pierce." (Lk. 2:35)

*February 3 — St. Blaise
Prayer: "O glorious St. Blaise, pray for us." (*Raccolta*, 537)

February 11 — Our Lady of Lourdes
Prayer: "O Mary, conceived without sin, pray for us who have recourse to thee." (*Raccolta*, 357)

*Lent — Ash Wednesday

STUDY LESSON FOR ASH WEDNESDAY

> "Remember, man, that thou art dust and unto dust thou shalt return" (Gen. 3:19).
> Blackboard

I. SUBJECT MATTER
Ash Wednesday — Lent

II. TYPE
Development

III. OBJECTIVES
A. To give an understanding of the holy season of Lent.
B. To lead the children to the proper observance of Lent.

---
* *Feasts to be developed thoroughly: lesson plans for each have been worked out and will be found on the following pages.*

IV. MATERIALS
None

V. PROCEDURE
A. Approach
Call attention to today's feast. Ask for meaning.

B. Presentation
1. Explanation and discussion:
   a) Explain the meaning of Lent — how it begins, how long it lasts, how Church celebrates, how we celebrate it.
   b) Explain the origin of the ashes which we receive on that day, also the purpose.
   c) Discuss proper penances and good works for Lent.
2. Organization:
   List with the children proper penances and good works which they can perform.
3. Application:
   The children formulate good Lenten resolutions.
4. Broader Appreciation:
   The children memorize the prayer, "Remember, man, that thou art dust."
5. Suggested Activity:
   The children write down their Lenten resolutions and then check daily to see if they are being carried out.

STUDY LESSON FOR THE FEAST OF ST. BLAISE

I. SUBJECT MATTER
Feast of St. Blaise

II. TYPE
Development

III. OBJECTIVES
A. To explain how the Church celebrates this feast.
B. To lead the children to an appreciation of the help the saints can give.
C. To lead the children to call upon St. Blaise for help against diseases of the throat.

IV. MATERIALS
A. Approach
Discuss: why will the priest bless more candles tomorrow?

B. Presentation
1. Explanation and discussion:
   a) Explain the origin of the feast of St. Blaise.
   b) Explain how the Church celebrates this feast.
   c) Explain and discuss the reason for throat blessings on this day.
2. Application:
   The children get their throats blessed.
3. Organization:
   The children list special saints who help us in special ways, e.g.:

a) St. Christopher protects us when traveling.
   b) St. Agatha protects us against fire.
   c) St. Joseph helps us die happily.
4. Broader Appreciation:
   Recite for the children the prayer said by the priest when he blesses the candles on the feast of St. Blaise.
5. Suggested Activity:
   The children take the responsibility of seeing that all the members of their family get their throats blessed.

After each Unit reteach and retest where there are weaknesses revealed.

CORRELATED ACTIVITIES FOR UNIT FOUR

Art
1. The children make Passion posters, crosses, symbols of suffering, etc.
2. The children collect pictures of the Passion and put them into sequential order in a book.
3. Picture study: "Jesus Carrying His Cross."
4. The children make a movie of the glorified life of Christ.

Music
1. Hymns:
   a) God of Mercy and Compassion, *St. Gregory Hymnal*, p. 134.
   b) Parce Domine, *St. Gregory Hymnal*, p. 239.
   c) The Sorrowful Mysteries, *People's Hymnal*, No. R-16.
   d) The Glorious Mysteries, *People's Hymnal*, No. R-17.
   e) Hail Holy Queen Enthroned Above, *People's Hymnal*, No. R-8.

English
1. The children write original prayers to be said while making the Stations of the Cross.
2. The children dramatize any stories taken in this Unit.
3. The children write original stories, poems, letters, or reports about topics of this Unit.

Science
The children plan a unit on water in our Lord's life.

UNIT FIVE. GOD THE HOLY GHOST COMES TO DO HIS WORK

(Text, *God's Truths Help Us Live*, pp. 177–210)

(Revised Baltimore Catechism No. 1 [Confraternity], Questions 53–64.)

INTRODUCTORY MATERIAL

I. INTRODUCTION FOR THE TEACHER

This unit is presented to acquaint the children with the third Person of the Blessed Trinity and His special gifts to us.

II. OBJECTIVES OF THE UNIT

A. To arouse in the children a desire to learn the story of grace, God's greatest gift to man.
B. To gain an understanding of the work of the Holy Spirit in applying to men the merits gained by the sufferings and death of Christ.

III. SUBJECT MATTER

A. Jesus sends the Holy Ghost.
B. The work of the Holy Ghost in us.
  1. The Holy Ghost gives us grace.
     a) What grace is.
     b) Kinds of grace.
     c) How we obtain grace.
     d) Chief powers the Holy Ghost gives us with His grace.

IV. TEACHER REFERENCES FOR UNIT FIVE

1. Baierl, *The Creed Explained*, pp. 349–386.
2. Belger, *Sing a Song of Holy Things*, pp. 45, 50, 53.
3. Brennan, *Angel Food*, pp. 23–25, 26–29.
4. Johnson, *Bible Story*, pp. 179–180, 190–191.
5. Kelly, *Baltimore Catechism No. 1, With Dev.*, pp. 64–178.
6. Lovasik, *Catechism Sketched*, pp. 27–49.
7. Montani, *St. Gregory Hymnal*, pp. 34, 35, 145.
8. Thayer, *The Child on His Knees*, pp. 12–13, 119, 122.

LESSON PLANS FOR UNIT FIVE

I. Introduction to Unit Five

God the Holy Ghost Comes to Do His Work. Text, p. 177

LESSON PLAN 115

I. SUBJECT MATTER
God the Holy Ghost Comes to Do His Work

II. TYPE
Introduction

III. MATERIALS
Unit Five, p. 177, in the children's text.

IV. PROCEDURE
Same as for introductory lesson for Unit Two, Lesson I, in Manual.

II. Work Study Periods for Unit Five
(Lessons 116–138)

UNIT FIVE, PART 1, Jesus Sends the Holy Ghost. Text, p. 178

LESSON PLAN 116

> "And they were all filled with the Holy Spirit" (Acts 2:4).
>
> Blackboard

I. SUBJECT MATTER
Jesus Sends the Holy Ghost

II. TYPE
Development

III. OBJECTIVES

A. To develop the story of the first Pentecost.
B. To acquaint the children with the work of the Apostles.
C. To inspire reverence for those who are now doing the work of the Apostles.
D. To lead the children to become "little apostles."

IV. MATERIALS
Poem — "Tell Me What," Thayer, *The Child on His Knees*, p. 119.
Picture — Descent of the Holy Ghost.

V. PROCEDURE

A. Approach
Recall our Lord's promise to the Apostles, "I will send the Holy Spirit to you."

B. Presentation
1. Explanation and discussion:
   a) Show picture and tell vividly the story of the descent of the Holy Ghost.
   b) Discuss: form the Holy Ghost took; gifts He brought; change in the Apostles.
   c) Tell incident of Peter's first sermon and the baptism of three thousand.
   d) Explain reason for calling Pentecost the birthday of the Church.
   e) Explain briefly how the Apostles followed the command: "Go and teach all nations."
   f) Give incidents in the lives of the Apostles to show how the Holy Spirit helped them in their work and sufferings.
   g) Explain briefly and discuss how the work of the Apostles continues today. Discuss respect we should have for those who do God's work today.
   h) End the presentation by repeating exact answer of the Revised Baltimore Catechism No. 1 (Confraternity), question 53, Text, p. 206.
2. Application:
The children resolve to be "little apostles" by helping others know about God.
3. Organization:
   a) How long did the Apostles have to wait for the coming of the Holy Ghost?
   b) On what day did the Holy Ghost come down upon the Apostles?
   c) How did the Apostles know when the Holy Spirit had come?
   d) What gifts did the Holy Ghost bring with Him?
   e) Why is Pentecost called the birthday of the Church?
4. Broader Appreciation:
Poem — "Tell Me What," Thayer, *The Child on His Knees*, p. 119.
5. Assignment:
Catechism question 53, p. 206, at the end of Unit Five in children's text.
6. Suggested Activity:
The children draw pictures to show some of the work that the Apostles did.

UNIT FIVE, PART 1 (cont.).

LESSON PLAN 117

Children read or reread and discuss Unit Five, Part 1, p. 178, in their text.

UNIT FIVE, PART 2, LESSON PLANS 118–119, The Holy Ghost Gives Us Grace. Text, p. 181

LESSON PLAN 118

> *"You shall be holy, for I am holy"* (Lev. 11:14).
> Blackboard

I. SUBJECT MATTER
The Holy Ghost Gives Us Grace

II. TYPE
Development

III. OBJECTIVES
A. To develop the knowledge of what sanctifying grace is and does.
B. To teach the children proper respect for all people.
C. To create in the children the desire to preserve sanctifying grace in them.

IV. MATERIALS
Story — "The White Ribbon," Brennan, *Angel Food*, pp. 23–25.

V. PROCEDURE

A. Approach
Discuss: Who is the Holy Ghost? What other names does He have? Where does He live? When did He first come to live in us?

B. Presentation
1. Explanation and discussion:
   a) Explain and discuss the work of the Holy Ghost in us — to make us holy with His grace. Define the term: grace (a supernatural gift from God which we need to get to heaven.) Define the term: supernatural gift; contrast with natural gifts.
   b) Give the names of the two kinds of grace — sanctifying grace and actual grace. Explain that we will learn about sanctifying grace first.
   c) Explain what sanctifying grace is — a supernatural gift from God which gives us supernatural life; that is, it allows us to share in God's own life. Define the term: supernatural life; contrast with natural life.
   d) Explain what sanctifying grace does; elaborate:
      1) Makes us holy and pleasing to God — like a precious jewel.
      2) Makes us adopted children of God — all of us are brothers and sisters.
      3) Makes us temples of the Holy Ghost — all kinds and colors of people may become temples.
      4) Gives us the right to go to heaven — no one enters heaven without it; tell briefly

the Bible story of the man not having on a wedding garment when he went to a feast.

    5) Gives us a new life, a supernatural life of the soul, which makes us like God, partakes of his nature, receives power to act like Him; holy, merciful, truthful, pure.

  e) End the presentation by repeating exact answers of the Revised Baltimore Catechism No. 1 (Confraternity), questions 54, 55, Text, p. 206.

2. Application:
What is the most precious gift we have? Why? Should we ever want to lose it? The children resolve to keep their souls and bodies pure and holy temples of the Holy Ghost.

3. Organization:
List on the board with the children ways in which we show that we are temples of the Holy Ghost.

4. Broader Appreciation:
Story — "The White Ribbon," Brennan, *Angel Food*, pp. 23–25.

5. Assignment:
Catechism questions 54 and 55, p. 206, at the end of Unit Five in children's text.

6. Suggested Activity:
The children draw pictures to show how to treat other children as brothers and sisters.

LESSON PLAN 119

Children read or reread and discuss Unit Five, Part 2, p. 181, in their text.

UNIT FIVE, PART 3, LESSON PLANS 120–121, The Holy Ghost Makes Us Holy — Sanctifying Grace. Text, p. 184

LESSON PLAN 120

> "Glory be to the Father, and to the Son, and to the Holy Ghost..."
> **Blackboard**

I. SUBJECT MATTER
Why We Need Sanctifying Grace; How We Might Lose It

II. TYPE
Development

III. OBJECTIVES
A. To give further understanding of sanctifying grace.
B. To give the children an appreciation of the great gift of sanctifying grace.
C. To lead the children to make all their acts count for heaven.

IV. MATERIALS
Poem — "Presents," Thayer, *The Child on His Knees*, p. 92.

V. PROCEDURE

A. Approach
Discuss: Do you think that sanctifying grace is necessary? Why?

B. Presentation
1. Explanation and discussion:
  a) Explain why we need sanctifying grace in our souls:
    1) To live with God in heaven some day; recall the parable of the wedding garment; recall that it is the only necessary thing to get us to heaven.
    2) To make our acts count for heaven — explain the difference between natural and supernatural acts. Explain how to make supernatural acts out of natural ones. Explain the use of a morning offering of all our acts.
  b) Explain and discuss how we lose sanctifying grace and how we regain it.
  c) Discuss the evils of mortal sin.
    1) Compare a person in mortal sin to a dead plant.
    2) Show how no acts count for heaven while we are in mortal sin.
  d) End the presentation by repeating exact answer of the Revised Baltimore Catechism No. 1 (Confraternity), question 56, Text, p. 206.

2. Application:
The children resolve to make every day one of doing supernatural acts all day long. The children resolve never to commit a mortal sin.

3. Organization:
  a) What is sanctifying grace?
  b) What does it do for us?
  c) Why do we need it?
  d) Why and how do we lose it?
  e) How can we get it back?

4. Broader Appreciation:
Poem — "Presents," Thayer, *The Child on His Knees*, p. 92.

5. Assignment:
Catechism question 56, p. 206, at the end of Unit Five in children's text.

6. Suggested Activity:
The children write an original composition on "Why Sanctifying Grace Is a Great Gift From God."

UNIT FIVE, PART 3 (cont.).

LESSON PLAN 121

The children read or reread and discuss Unit Five, Part 3, p. 184, in their text.

UNIT FIVE, PART 4, LESSON PLANS 122–124, Actual Grace. Text, p. 188.

LESSON PLAN 122

> Without God, I can do nothing.
> Blackboard

I. SUBJECT MATTER
What Actual Grace Is and Does

II. TYPE
Development

III. OBJECTIVES
A. To develop an understanding and appreciation of actual grace.
B. To lead the children to use actual graces.

IV. MATERIALS
Poem — "What To Do," Thayer, *The Child on His Knees*, p. 122.

V. PROCEDURE

A. Approach
What is sanctifying grace? Why is it necessary?

B. Presentation
1. Explanation and discussion:
   a) Explain that God has given us another great gift to help us keep our sanctifying grace.
   b) Explain what actual grace is — a supernatural help that God gives when we need it; explain that this grace differs from sanctifying grace because it comes as we need it; we do not have to take it.
   c) Explain what actual grace does:
      1) Enlightens our mind and strengthens our will.
         (a) Give many examples of actual grace at work — in the doing of good acts and in fighting temptation; also give examples of refusing actual grace.
         (b) The children give examples of times when actual grace helped them.
         (c) The children suggest times during the day when the help of the Holy Ghost is needed most.
2. Application:
   The children resolve to use God's actual grace whenever He sends it to them.

3. Organization:
   a) What is actual grace?
   b) What does it do for us?
   c) When does actual grace come to us?
4. Broader Appreciation:
   Poem — "What To Do," Thayer, *The Child on His Knees*, p. 122.
5. Assignment:
   None
6. Suggested Activity:
   The children draw pictures of themselves using God's actual grace.

UNIT FIVE, PART 6 (cont.).

LESSON PLAN 123

> — "Let us praise and thank the Holy Spirit" (Raccolta, 330).
> Blackboard

I. SUBJECT MATTER
Why We Need God's Actual Grace

II. TYPE
Development

III. OBJECTIVES
A. To further develop the children's understanding of actual grace.
B. To create the desire to please God always by our actions.
C. To lead the children to invoke the Holy Spirit when they need His help.

IV. MATERIALS
Poem — "God's Help," Sister Josita Belger, *Sing a Song of Holy Things*, p. 50.

V. PROCEDURE

A. Approach
Discuss: What is actual grace? When does God give it to us?

B. Presentation
1. Explanation and discussion:
   a) Explain the necessity for actual grace.
      1) Without it we could not keep sanctifying grace.
      2) We need it to do good and avoid evil.
      3) We need it because Christ has said, "Without me, you can do nothing."
   b) Cite examples of times when we need God's actual grace the most.
   c) Explain how we lose God's actual grace:
      1) By not accepting it when God offers it to us — give many examples because this is so necessary.

d) Remind the children that the sacraments of Penance and Holy Eucharist give us many actual graces to do good and avoid evil.
   e) End the presentation by repeating exact answer of the Revised Baltimore Catechism No. 1 (Confraternity), question 57, Text, p. 207.
  2. Application:
  The children resolve to rely upon the Holy Ghost's help whenever they need it.
  3. Organization:
  The children tell how actual grace helped them avoid evil and do good in their lives.
  4. Broader Appreciation:
  Poem — "God's Help," Sister Josita Belger, *Sing a Song of Holy Things*, p. 50.
  5. Assignment:
  Catechism question 57, p. 207, at the end of Unit Five in the children's text.
  6. Suggested Activity:
  The children make up a little prayer to thank God the Holy Ghost for His goodness in making them holy.

UNIT FIVE, PART 4 (cont.).

LESSON PLAN 124

The children read or reread and discuss Unit Five, Part 4, p. 188, in their text.

UNIT FIVE, PART 5, LESSON PLANS 125–126, How We Obtain Grace. Text, p. 191

LESSON PLAN 125

"O Lord, make haste to help me" (Raccolta, 20).
Blackboard

I. **SUBJECT MATTER**
   How We Obtain Grace

II. **TYPE**
   Development

III. **OBJECTIVES**
   A. To develop a better understanding of the means of grace.
   B. To develop an attitude of gratitude to God for His grace.
   C. To lead the children to use God's means of grace frequently.

IV. **MATERIALS**
   Story — "Snow White and the Seven Dwarfs," Brennan, *Angel Food*, pp. 26–29.
   Pictures — Seven Sacraments.

V. **PROCEDURE**
  A. Approach
  Discuss: When did you first begin to live your supernatural life? How?
  B. Presentation
  1. Explanation and discussion:
   a) Explain that at baptism the Holy Ghost gave us enough grace to get to heaven; God gives us many ways in which to get more grace so as to earn a higher place in heaven.
   b) Explain the ways of gaining grace:
    1) Through prayer.
     (a) List with the children the times when prayer is needed.
     (b) Discuss the saying of Jesus — "Pray always."
     (c) Give a chalk talk illustrating prayer as rain to help the plant of grace grow in us. Show what happens when this plant is not watered.
    2) Through the sacraments.
     (a) Give the names of each of the seven sacraments and the effects of each sacrament. Show pictures.
     (b) Give a chalk talk on the seven rivers of grace.
    3) Through good works.
     (a) Practicing supernatural virtues.
     (b) Works of mercy.
     (c) End the presentation by repeating exact answer of the Revised Baltimore Catechism No. 1 (Confraternity), question 58, Text, p. 207.
  2. Application:
  The children resolve to use every possible means of grace so as to increase in grace daily. Stress the frequent use of penance and the Holy Eucharist.
  3. Organization:
   a) What are some ways of getting grace?
   b) When should we pray?
   c) What are the names of the seven sacraments?
   d) Which sacraments can you receive many times so as to get grace over and over again?
   e) What good works gain grace?
  4. Broader Appreciation:
  Story — "Snow White and the Seven Dwarfs," Brennan, *Angel Food*, pp. 26–29.
  5. Assignment:
  Catechism question 58, p. 207, at the end of Unit Five in the children's text.
  6. Suggested Activity:
  The children bring two plants to school — one to be watered and one to be given no water. Label the plants "Us." Show how the water will make one plant grow.

UNIT FIVE, PART 5 (cont.).

LESSON PLAN 126

The children read or reread and discuss Unit 5, Part 5, p. 191, in their text.

UNIT FIVE, PART 6, The Virtues and Gifts of the Holy Ghost. Text, p. 193

LESSON PLAN 127

I. SUBJECT MATTER
The Holy Ghost Makes Us Holy

II. TYPE
Discussion

III. MATERIALS
Children's text, Unit Five — Parts 1, 2, 3, 4, and 5, pp. 178–193.

IV. PROCEDURE
Same as for discussion plan Unit One, Lesson 8, p. 13, in the Manual.

UNIT FIVE, PART 7, LESSON PLANS 128–129, Faith. Text, p. 196

LESSON PLAN 128

> "Without faith it is impossible to please God" (Hebr. 11:6).
>
> Blackboard

I. SUBJECT MATTER
Powers With Grace — Faith

II. TYPE
Development

III. OBJECTIVES
A. To give knowledge of the special powers which the Holy Ghost gives us with His grace.
B. To instill in the children a love for their faith and the desire to practice it.

IV. MATERIALS
None

V. PROCEDURE

A. Approach
We have learned many wonderful things that the Holy Ghost does for us. Today we will find out that the Holy Ghost does even more for us.

B. Presentation

1. Explanation and discussion:
   a) Explain that when the Holy Ghost came at baptism, He brought with sanctifying grace some supernatural gifts or powers to help us know, love, and serve God better.
   b) Give the names of the three theological virtues — faith, hope, and charity. Explain the term: theological virtues. Show symbols for each. Explain what they are: power to believe in God, power to hope in God, power to love God.
   c) Mention but do not explain the seven gifts of the Holy Ghost which will be studied next year.
   d) Explain and discuss the virtue of faith — good habit of believing in God and the things He has made known to us. (God can't lie, so we take His word for what He teaches us through the Catholic Church.)
   e) Explain that we must believe all that the Catholic Church teaches or we can't get to heaven — even if we can't understand some of these truths, e.g., Blessed Trinity.
   f) Explain that faith is a very special gift — necessary to get to heaven; we must be willing to die rather than lose it. Cite examples of martyrs and their reward for keeping faith.
   g) Compare faith with a muscle — we must exercise and strengthen it or it will be useless or lost. Discuss ways of practicing and strengthening faith:
      1) Prayer (stress act of faith).
      2) Study of our religion.
      3) Reading of holy books.
      4) Listening to sermons.
   h) Explain and discuss ways of losing faith:
      1) Not praying for a long time.
      2) Listening to non-Catholic sermons (can be dangerous).
      3) Not believing all that the Church teaches.
   i) End the presentation by repeating exact answers of the Revised Baltimore Catechism No. 1 (Confraternity), questions, 59, 60, 61, 64, Text, pp. 207–208.

2. Application:
The children resolve to guard, love, and strengthen faith.

3. Organization:
   a) What special powers did the Holy Ghost give you with sanctifying grace?
   b) What are the three theological virtues?
   c) What is the virtue of faith?
   d) How do we practice our faith?
   e) Why must we believe all that the Catholic Church teaches?

4. Broader Appreciation:
The children recite the "Act of Faith."

5. Assignment:
Catechism questions 59, 60, 61, 64, pp. 207, 208, at the end of Unit Five in the children's text.
6. Suggested Activity:
The children make an original act of faith.

UNIT FIVE, PART 7 (cont.).

LESSON PLAN 129

The children read or reread and discuss Unit Five, Parts 6 and 7, pp. 193–198, in their text.

UNIT FIVE, PART 8, LESSON PLANS 130–131, Hope. Text, p. 198

LESSON PLAN 130

> "I have hoped in the mercy of God forever" (Ps. 51:10).
> Blackboard

I. SUBJECT MATTER
The Virtue of Hope

II. TYPE
Development

III. OBJECTIVES
A. To give the children an understanding of the virtue of hope.
B. To lead the children to trust in God's mercy.
C. To lead the children to do and accept willingly God's holy will in all things.

IV. MATERIALS
None

V. PROCEDURE

A. Approach
Recall names and symbols of three theological virtues. Recall briefly what faith is, how increased.

B. Presentation
1. Explanation and discussion:
   a) Explain and discuss the meaning of the virtue of hope — trust in God's mercy and help.
   b) Explain the necessity for this virtue — need it to get to heaven; contrast Peter's trust with Judas' loss of hope; St. Maria Goretti's hope in God.
   c) Explain and discuss ways in which hope must be practiced:
      1) Prayer and sacraments.
      2) Resignation to God's will.
      3) Starting anew each day.
      4) Never getting discouraged.
   d) Explain and discuss ways of losing hope:
      1) Never doing anything to show we want to go to heaven.
      2) Giving up hope of God's mercy and help.
   e) End the presentation by repeating exact answer of the Revised Baltimore Catechism No. 1 (Confraternity), question 62, Text, p. 208.
2. Application:
Children resolve to look upon God as a loving Father who will take care of all their needs for body and soul if they trust Him.
3. Organization:
   a) What is the virtue of hope?
   b) What is the symbol for the virtue of hope?
   c) Why must we practice the virtue of hope?
4. Broader Appreciation:
The children recite the "Act of Hope."
5. Assignment:
Catechism question 62, p. 208, at the end of Unit Five in the children's text.
6. Suggested Activity:
With the prayer, "Heart of Jesus, I put my trust in Thee," and a holy picture, the children construct a small shrine.

UNIT FIVE, PART 8 (cont.).

LESSON PLAN 131

The children read or reread and discuss Unit Five, Part 8, p. 198, in their text.

UNIT FIVE, PART 9, LESSON PLANS 132–136, Charity. Text, p. 201

LESSON PLAN 132

> "Thou shalt love the Lord thy God . . ." (Mt. 22:37).
> Blackboard

I. SUBJECT MATTER
The Virtue of Love

II. TYPE
Development

III. OBJECTIVES
A. To develop the virtue of love in theory and in practice.
B. To show the children how loving my neighbor is loving God.

IV. MATERIALS
Poem — "Faith, Hope, Love," Sister Josita Belger, *Sing a Song of Holy Things*, p. 45.

V. PROCEDURE

A. Approach
Today we shall talk about the greatest of all virtues.

B. Presentation
1. Explanation and discussion:
   a) Explain the virtue of charity — love of God and love of neighbor for the love of God. Define term: neighbor.
   b) Explain that love is expressed best by doing. Explain and discuss how love is practiced:
      1) Mass, Holy Communion, prayer — Act of Love.
      2) Keeping commandments.
      3) Loving and helping neighbor — forgetting self to make others happy — be specific.
      4) Seeing Christ in everyone — "What you do to others . . ."; be specific.
   c) Explain and discuss how charity is lost:
      1) Losing sanctifying grace.
      2) Neglecting our duties toward God and neighbor.
      3) Thinking only of self.
   d) Explain why charity is called the greatest of all virtues.
   e) End the presentation by repeating exact answer of the Revised Baltimore Catechism No. 1 (Confraternity), question 63, Text, p. 208.
2. Application:
   The children resolve to grow daily in love of God and neighbor.
3. Organization:
   List with the children ways of showing love for God and love for neighbor.
4. Broader Appreciation:
   Poem — "Faith, Hope, Love," Sister Josita Belger, *Sing a Song of Holy Things*, p. 45.
5. Assignment:
   Catechism question 63, p. 208, at the end of Unit Five in the children's text.
6. Suggested Activity:
   The children write an original prayer to tell God that they love Him.

UNIT FIVE, PART 9 (cont.).

LESSON PLAN 133

> "O my God, I love You above all things"
> (Act of Love).
>
> Blackboard

I. SUBJECT MATTER
Act of Love

II. TYPE
Development

III. MATERIALS
Prayer — "Act of Love," p. 3 in the children's text.

IV. PROCEDURE
See plan for "Act of Faith," Unit Two, Lesson 6 in the Manual.

UNIT FIVE, PART 9 (cont.).

LESSON PLAN 134

The children read or reread and discuss Unit Five, Part 9, p. 201, in their text.

UNIT FIVE, PART 9 (cont.).

LESSON PLAN 135

I. SUBJECT MATTER
God the Holy Ghost Comes to Do His Work

II. TYPE
Discussion

III. MATERIALS
Children's text, "Problems" at the end of Unit Five, Part 9, p. 204.

IV. PROCEDURE
See plan for discussion, Unit One, Lesson 8, p. 27, in the Manual.

UNIT FIVE, PART 9 (cont.).

LESSON PLAN 136

I. SUBJECT MATTER
God the Holy Ghost Comes to Do His Work

II. TYPE
Drill

III. MATERIALS
Questions at the end of Unit Five, pp. 205–206, in the children's text.

IV. PROCEDURE
Same as for drill lesson Unit One, Lesson 21, p. 41, in the Manual.

III. Culmination of Unit Five

LESSON PLAN 137

I. SUBJECT MATTER
God the Holy Ghost Comes to Do His Work

II. TYPE
Culmination

III. MATERIALS

Hymns, poems, stories, etc., developed during this unit.

IV. PROCEDURE

Same as for culmination lesson for Unit One, Lesson 22, p. 19, in Manual.

IV. Evaluation of Unit Five

LESSON PLAN 138

The children take the written test found at the end of Unit Five, pp. 208–210, in their text. After each Unit reteach and retest where there are weaknesses revealed.

CORRELATED ACTIVITIES FOR UNIT FIVE

Art
1. The children make symbols of the Holy Ghost.
2. The children make large pictures to illustrate the seven sacraments.
3. The children make block print symbols of faith, hope, and charity.

Music
1. Hymns:
   a) Come, Holy Ghost, *St. Gregory Hymnal*, p. 35.
   b) Acts of Faith, Hope, and Charity, *St. Gregory Hymnal*, p. 145.
   c) Holy Spirit, Lord of Light, *St. Gregory Hymnal*, p. 34.

English
1. The children dramatize any stories taken in this unit.
2. The children memorize any poem taken in this unit.
3. The children write original stories or poems about topics in this unit.

Science

The children plan a unit on weather.

UNIT SIX. THE WORK OF THE HOLY GHOST IN THE CHURCH

(Text, *God's Truths Help Us Live*, pp. 211–240)

(Revised Baltimore Catechism No. 1 [Confraternity], Questions 65–83.)

INTRODUCTORY MATERIAL

I. INTRODUCTION FOR THE TEACHER

This unit is presented to acquaint the children with the work of the Holy Spirit here on earth, namely: the spiritual guidance of the Catholic Church, and the sanctification of its members.

II. OBJECTIVES OF THE UNIT

A. To foster the attitude of reverence, obedience, and appreciation toward the Catholic Church and its leaders.
B. To show by our daily actions a realization of the indwelling of the Holy Spirit.

III. SUBJECT MATTER

A. The work of the Holy Ghost in the Church
  1. What the Church is
  2. Why the Church was started
  3. The rulers of the Church
  4. The marks of the Church
  5. The members of the Church
B. What the Church teaches about life everlasting
  1. Particular Judgment
  2. General Judgment

IV. TEACHER REFERENCES FOR UNIT SIX

1. Baierl, *The Creed Explained*, pp. 387–572.
2. Belger, *Sing a Song of Holy Things*, pp. 40, 42 and 43, 100 and 101.
3. Johnson, *Bible Story*, pp. 225–226.
4. Kelly, *Baltimore Catechism No. 1, With Dev.*, pp. 269–282.
5. Lovasik, *Catechism Sketched*, pp. 65–127.
6. Montani, *St. Gregory Hymnal*, pp. 121, 122, 199.
7. Thayer, *The Child on His Knees*, pp. 103, 110, 115, 73, 74, 79.

LESSON PLANS FOR UNIT SIX

I. Introduction to Unit Six

The Work of the Holy Ghost in the Church. Text, p. 211

LESSON PLAN 139

I. **SUBJECT MATTER**
The Work of the Holy Ghost in the Church

II. **TYPE**
Introduction

III. **MATERIALS**
Unit Six, p. 211, in children's text.

IV. **PROCEDURE**
Same as for introductory lesson, Unit Two, Lesson 24, p. 22, in the Manual.

II. Work Study Periods for Unit Six
(Lesson Plans 140–159)

UNIT SIX PART 1, The Holy Ghost and the Church. Text, p. 212

LESSON PLAN 140

> "I believe in the Holy, Catholic Church" (Creed).
> Blackboard

I. **SUBJECT MATTER**
The Catholic Church

II. **TYPE**
Development

III. **OBJECTIVES**
A. To lead children to an understanding of what the Church is.
B. To give the children an appreciation of the wonderful gift of faith that is theirs.
C. To lead the children to the desire to be good, holy members of the Church.

IV. **MATERIALS**
Poem: "Trading," Thayer, *The Child on His Knees*, p. 130.

V. PROCEDURE

A. Approach

When you hear the words: "Catholic Church" what do you think of?

B. Presentation

1. Explanation and discussion:
    a) Explain that the word Church does not mean building; it is like a big family — all the people in a family are related. In the family, all members love each other; if one is bad, all suffer.
    b) Explain why the (Catholic) Church is like a big family (or congregation):
        1) It is made up of all baptized persons who:
            (*a*) Have the same true faith.
            (*b*) Have the same sacrifice.
            (*c*) Have the same sacraments.
            (*d*) Have the same spiritual rulers — Jesus is invisible ruler, pope is visible ruler. Define terms: invisible and visible.
    c) Elaborate on each point above (a, b, c, d).
    d) Explain that this family — the Church — is happy when some member does good, is shamed when one member is bad. (Cite examples.)
    e) Explain that many people do not belong to the Catholic Church, so we should pray every day that all people, especially those dear to us, will join the Catholic Church.
    f) Explain that the Catholic Church is like a body — Christ the head; we the members.
    g) End the presentation by repeating exact answer of the Revised Baltimore Catechism No. 1 (Confraternity), question 65, Text, p. 235.

2. Application:
    The children resolve to thank God every day that they are members of His (Catholic) Church, and to try to be good, faithful members of this (Catholic) Church.

3. Organization:
    List with children ways in which we show that we are good members of the Catholic Church.

4. Broader Appreciation:
    Poem: "Trading," Thayer, *The Child on His Knees*, p. 130.

5. Assignment:
    Catechism question 65, p. 235, at end of Unit Six in the children's text.

6. Suggested Activity:
    The children make a frieze to illustrate how all Catholics are united.

UNIT SIX, PART 1 (cont.).

LESSON PLAN 141

> "You shall be holy, for I am holy" (Lev. 11:14).
> Blackboard

I. SUBJECT MATTER
Why Jesus Started the Church

II. TYPE
Development

III. OBJECTIVES
A. To give an understanding of why the Church was founded.
B. To instill in the children the desire to use the helps to heaven which the Catholic Church gives.
C. To give the children an appreciation of what the Catholic Church does for them.

IV. MATERIALS
Poem: "If I Were You," Thayer, *The Child on His Knees*, p. 110.

V. PROCEDURE

A. Approach
What is the Church? Who started it?

B. Presentation
1. Explanation and discussion:
    a) Explain and discuss why Jesus started the Catholic Church:
        1) To teach us; discuss some of the truths the Church teaches.
        2) To make laws to guide us; discuss some of the laws of the Church.
        3) To make us holy; discuss ways in which the Church makes us holy.
        4) To save us; explain that we can be saved only by being good members of the Church; explain how non-Catholics can be saved.
    b) End the presentation by repeating exact answer to the Revised Baltimore Catechism No. 1 (Confraternity), question 66, Text, p. 235.

2. Application:
    How can we be sure to get to heaven? The children resolve to make themselves holy members of the Church by doing and believing what the Church teaches.

3. Organization:
    Make a simple outline with the class:
    a) Why Jesus started the Church:
        1) To teach us.
        2) To make laws to guide us.
        3) To make us holy.
        4) To save us.

4. Broader Appreciation:
Poem: "If I Were You," Thayer, *The Child on His Knees*, p. 110.
5. Assignment:
Catechism question 66, p. 235, at the end of Unit Six in children's text.
6. Suggested Activity:
The children write a letter to a friend, explaining why Jesus started the Catholic Church.

UNIT SIX, PART 1 (cont.).

LESSON PLAN 142

The children read or reread and discuss Unit Six, Part 1, p. 212, in their text.

UNIT SIX, PART 2, LESSON PLANS 142–143, The Rulers of the Church. Text, p. 215

LESSON PLAN 143

> "Upon this rock I will build My Church" (Mt. 26:18).
> Blackboard

I. **SUBJECT MATTER**
The Rulers of the Church

II. **TYPE**
Development

III. **OBJECTIVES**
  A. To give the children a knowledge of the work of the rulers of the Church.
  B. To inspire reverence for and obedience to the Church's rulers.

IV. **MATERIALS**
Poem: "The Catholic Church," Sister Josita Belger, *Sing a Song of Holy Things*, p. 40.

V. **PROCEDURE**
  A. **Approach**
  Who started the Catholic Church?

  B. **Presentation**
  1. Explanation and discussion:
     a) Recall the fact that Jesus started the Church to teach, sanctify, and rule us. Explain that in the Church, He would remain the invisible Head, but would give His powers to teach, sanctify, and rule to the Apostles and their successors. (Explain the term: successors.) Recall incidents in which these powers were given to the Apostles:
        1) To teach — "Going, therefore, teach."
        2) To sanctify — "Whose sins . . . ," "Do this in remembrance . . ."
        3) To rule — "Whatsoever you bind upon earth . . ."
     b) Explain that the Apostles were made bishops so they could pass their powers on to other priests.
     c) Explain that the Apostles needed one chief ruler and teacher to take our Lord's place in guiding them in their work; tell incident in which Peter became the first pope — the visible head of the Church.
     d) Explain and discuss the rulers of the Church today; show pictures:
        1) Pope
           (a) Explain why he is called the successor of St. Peter.
           (b) Explain titles: visible head of Church, Bishop of Rome, Holy Father.
           (c) Discuss name of present pope, popes that children know.
           (d) Explain briefly and simply infallibility of pope.
           (e) Discuss work in Church.
        2) Bishops
           (a) Explain why they are called the successors of the Apostles.
           (b) Discuss name of present bishop; work he does for men.
           (c) Explain briefly how he is chosen.
           (d) Explain that bishop must obey pope and we must obey bishop.
           (e) End the presentation by repeating exact answers of the Revised Baltimore Catechism No. 1 (Confraternity), questions 67–71, Text, pp. 235–236.
        3) Priests
           (a) Explain why they are called the bishop's helpers.
           (b) Discuss the work they do for men.
           (c) Discuss names of parish priests.
           (d) Explain that priests must obey bishop and we must obey priests.
           (e) Explain that priests are not successors to Apostles, but only bishops are.

  2. Application:
  Since the pope, the bishops, and priests are doing our Lord's work today, do they need our prayers? How should we treat them? The children resolve to pray for, love, obey, and respect Christ's representatives.

  3. Organization:
  List with the children some of the duties we owe to our parish priests.

  4. Broader Appreciation:
  Poem: "The Catholic Church," Sister Josita Belger, *Sing a Song of Holy Things*, p. 40.

5. Assignment:
Catechism questions 67, 68, 69, 70, 71, pp. 235–236, at the end of Unit Six in children's text.
6. Suggested Activity:
The children make up original prayers for the pope, bishop, or priests.

UNIT SIX, PART 2 (cont.).

LESSON PLAN 144

The children read or reread and discuss Unit Six, Part 2, p. 215, in their text.

UNIT SIX, PART 3, LESSON PLANS 145–148, The Marks of the Church. Text, pp. 219–221

LESSON PLAN 145

> "There shall be one fold and one shepherd" (Jn. 10:16).
>
> Blackboard

I. SUBJECT MATTER
The Marks of the Church — The Church Is One

II. TYPE
Development

III. OBJECTIVES
A. To give the children the knowledge that the Catholic Church is the one true Church.
B. To lead the children to appreciate their faith and to help others belong to the Catholic Church.

IV. MATERIALS
Picture: Good Shepherd.

V. PROCEDURE
A. Approach
As we look about us today, we find all kinds of churches — Catholic, Baptist, Methodist, etc. Were all these churches started by Christ?

B. Presentation
1. Explanation and discussion:
    a) Explain that Jesus started just one church — the Catholic Church; He wanted all people to belong to this one Church; He gave the Catholic Church four marks or signs to prove that this is the Church which He started; no other church has these marks, so we know that the Catholic Church is the true Church.
    b) Give the four marks of the Church — one, holy, catholic or universal, apostolic. Explain that we will talk about each mark in our religion classes.
    c) Explain the meaning: The Church is one:
        1) All Catholics have the same true faith (believe same things).
        2) All Catholics have the same seven sacraments.
        3) All Catholics have the same sacrifice — the Mass.
        4) All Catholics are united under the pope.
    d) Give examples to show how other churches are not united — if they would be truly united as we are, they would eventually become Catholics.
    e) Show picture of Good Shepherd and tell story to show that some day there will be but one fold and one shepherd.
    f) End the presentation by repeating exact answers of the Revised Baltimore Catechism No. 1 (Confraternity), questions 72, 73, Text, p. 236.
2. Application:
The children thank God that they belong to His sheepfold, and resolve to help others who are straying outside to come into the sheepfold.
3. Organization:
    a) What are the marks of the Church?
    b) Why did Jesus give His Church these four marks?
    c) How is the Church one?
4. Broader Appreciation:
The children make up a little thank-you prayer to the Good Shepherd for letting them be one of His sheep.
5. Assignment:
Catechism questions 72, 73, p. 236, at the end of Unit Six, in children's text.
6. Suggested Activity:
The children draw a picture to illustrate the story of the Good Shepherd.

UNIT SIX, PART 3 (cont.).

LESSON PLAN 146

> "He shall live with you and shall be in you" (Jn. 14:17).
>
> Blackboard

I. SUBJECT MATTER
The Church Is Holy

II. TYPE
Development

III. OBJECTIVES
A. To give the children an understanding that the Church is holy.
B. To create in the children the desire to use the means to holiness which the Church offers.

IV. **MATERIALS**

Poem: "Not Unless," Thayer, *The Child on His Knees*, p. 115.

V. **PROCEDURE**

A. **Approach**

How do you know that the Catholic Church is the true Church started by Jesus? Review briefly the mark: it is one.

B. **Presentation**

1. Explanation and discussion:
   a) Explain the second mark of the Church: it is holy:
      1) Jesus, who started the Church, is holy; Jesus started no other Church — rest were started by men (some of them were not holy).
      2) The Church gives us the sacraments to make us holy — we're expected to be holy members of the Church.
      3) Many people who belong to it are now saints in heaven — discuss.
2. Application:
   Since we belong to the holy Church of Christ we are expected to grow in holiness. Recall the helps to holiness which the Church gives. The children resolve to grow daily in holiness.
3. Organization:
   List with the children ways in which we can grow in holiness.
4. Broader Appreciation:
   Poem: "Not Unless," Thayer, *The Child on His Knees*, p. 115.
5. Assignment:
   None
6. Suggested Activity:
   The children write a letter to a friend explaining why the Catholic Church is holy.

UNIT SIX, PART 3 (cont.).

LESSON PLAN 147

"Going, therefore, teach ye all nations" (Mt. 28:19).
Blackboard

I. **SUBJECT MATTER**
The Church Is Catholic

II. **TYPE**
Development

III. **OBJECTIVES**

A. To teach the meaning of the term: catholic.
B. To give the children an appreciation of the Church as one for all kinds of people.
C. To lead the children to work for the salvation of all by prayer and sacrifice.

IV. **MATERIALS**

Poem: "Loving," Thayer, *The Child on His Knees*, pp. 73 and 74.

V. **PROCEDURE**

A. **Approach**

To which church do you belong? Why is it called the Catholic Church?

B. **Presentation**

1. Explanation and discussion:
   a) Explain that the Church is said to be catholic or universal because it is for all men at all times all over the world. Give examples. Explain how some churches are not universal.
   b) Refer to our Lord's command to the Apostles to teach *all* nations *all* truths at *all* times.
   c) Explain and discuss how this command is being carried on today:
      1) Work of missionaries.
      2) Trials and sufferings of missionaries.
      3) Ways we help missionaries.
         (a) Prayer.
         (b) Sacrifice.
   d) End the presentation by repeating exact answer of the Revised Baltimore Catechism No. 1 (Confraternity), question 74, Text, p. 236.
2. Application:
   Do you remember our Lord's promise that some day there will be but one fold and one Shepherd? What can you do now to help the missionaries make this promise come true?
3. Organization:
   a) Why is our Church called the Catholic Church?
   b) Who may belong to this Church?
   c) How do you know that our Lord wants everyone to belong to His Church?
   d) How can you help others become Catholics?
4. Broader Appreciation:
   Poem: "Loving," Thayer, *The Child on His Knees*, pp. 73, 74.
5. Assignment:
   Catechism question 74, p. 236, at the end of Unit Six in children's text.
6. Suggested Activity:
   The children make a large classroom frieze to show that all nations may belong to the Catholic Church.

UNIT SIX, PART 3 (cont.).

LESSON PLAN 148

"Upon this rock I will build my Church" (Mt. 26:18).
Blackboard

I. **SUBJECT MATTER**
The Church Is Apostolic

II. **TYPE**
Development

III. **OBJECTIVES**
A. To give the children an understanding of the fourth mark of the Church: the Church is apostolic.
B. To increase the children's appreciation of and love for their faith.

IV. **MATERIALS**
None

V. **PROCEDURE**

A. **Approach**
Review the marks of the Church briefly. Ask what the word "Apostolic" might mean.

B. **Presentation**
1. Explanation and discussion:
   a) Explain the term: Apostolic; show how the Church is Apostolic.
      1) Started with Christ and the Apostles; no other church can go back that far; cite origins of some non-Catholic churches.
      2) Continues through the popes who are the successors of St. Peter, and the bishops who are the successors of the Apostles; explain the unbroken line of rulers and apostolic powers.
      3) Teaches same truths that Jesus taught the Apostles; discuss some of these truths and tell how we learn these same truths today.
      4) End the presentation by repeating exact answer of the Revised Baltimore Catechism (Confraternity), question 75, Text, p. 236.
2. Application:
   Can you see, now, why the Catholic Church is the only true Church? Can you see why we must belong to it if we want to be saved? The children resolve to cling to their faith firmly.
3. Organization:
   a) What are the marks of the Church?
   b) How is the Church one?
   c) How is the Church holy?
   d) How is the Church catholic?
   e) How is the Church apostolic?
4. Broader Appreciation:
   The children recite the Apostles' Creed to tell God they believe the same truths that the Apostles believed and taught.
5. Assignment:
   Catechism question 75, p. 236, at the end of Unit Six in children's text.
6. Suggested Activity:
   Write a prayer to thank God for letting you be a member of the true Church.

UNIT SIX, PART 3 (cont.).

LESSON PLAN 149

The children read or reread and discuss Part 3, p. 219, in their text.

UNIT SIX, PART 4, LESSON PLANS 150–151, Communion of Saints — Forgiveness of Sins. Text, p. 223

LESSON PLAN 150

> "I believe in the communion of saints" (Creed).
> Blackboard

I. **SUBJECT MATTER**
The Members of the Church

II. **TYPE**
Development

III. **OBJECTIVES**
A. To acquaint the children with the communion of saints.
B. To lead the children to help and love the living and dead members of the Catholic Church.

IV. **MATERIALS**
Poem: "The Catholic Child," Sister Josita Belger, *Sing a Song of Holy Things*, pp. 42, 43.

V. **PROCEDURE**

A. **Approach**
Today you're going to find out that the Catholic Church has more members than you ever dreamed of.

B. **Presentation**
1. Explanation and discussion:
   a) Explain that the Catholic Church has three special — and very large — divisions, so that even after death we can still belong to the Catholic Church.
   b) Explain the communion of saints:
      1) Define phrase: communion of saints.
      2) Give names of three divisions of the Catholic Church and by means of chalk talk show how they help each other.
         (a) Souls in heaven.
            (1) Pray for those on earth.
            (2) Pray for souls in purgatory.

(b) Souls in purgatory.
   (1) Help those on earth after they reach heaven.
(c) People on earth.
   (1) Pray to saints in heaven.
   (2) Pray for souls in purgatory.
   (3) Pray for and help each other.

c) Explain that people in heaven and purgatory have had sins forgiven, people on earth know their sins can be forgiven, so we pray in the Apostles' Creed, "I believe in the forgiveness of sins."

d) Discuss: Are all kinds and colors of people in heaven?

e) End the presentation by repeating exact answers of the Revised Baltimore Catechism No. 1 (Confraternity), questions 76, 77, Text, p. 237.

2. Application:
The children resolve to help as many as possible become members of the (Catholic) Church on earth, and resolve to help the poor souls get to heaven.

3. Organization:
The children name the three divisions of the Catholic Church and tell how each division helps the others.

4. Broader Appreciation:
Poem: "The Catholic Child," Sister Josita Belger, *Sing a Song of Holy Things*, pp. 42–43.

5. Assignment:
Catechism questions 76 and 77, p. 237, at the end of Unit Six in children's text.

6. Suggested Activity:
The children draw a picture to show the three divisions of the Church.

UNIT SIX, PART 4 (cont.).

LESSON PLAN 151

The children read or reread and discuss Part 4, p. 223, in children's text.

UNIT SIX, PART 5, LESSON PLANS 152–153, What the Church Teaches About Life Everlasting — The Particular Judgment. Text, p. 227

LESSON PLAN 152

> "He who does the will of my Father in heaven shall enter the kingdom of heaven" (Mt. 7:21).
>
> Blackboard

I. SUBJECT MATTER
Particular Judgment

II. TYPE
Development

III. OBJECTIVES
A. To give an understanding of the particular judgment.
B. To lead the children to live good lives, so they will die happy deaths.
C. To lead the children to look upon death, not as something terrible, but as a calling to our reward.

IV. MATERIALS
Poem: "If I should Die," Thayer, *The Child on His Knees*, p. 79.

V. PROCEDURE

A. Approach
There is only one thing that everyone in this world has to do. Do you know what that one thing is? (Die.)

B. Presentation
1. Explanation and discussion:
   a) Explain and discuss the term: death. Discuss what happens to the body; why it must go back to dust.
   b) Explain and discuss what happens to the soul:
      1) Particular judgment:
         (a) What it is, where it takes place, who judges.
      2) How soul is rewarded or punished:
         (a) Heaven — who go there, how long they stay, what they do there.
         (b) Purgatory — who go there, how long they must stay, what they do there, what happens after soul is made perfect.
         (c) Hell — who go there; how long they must stay, what they do there.
         (d) End the presentation by repeating exact answers of the Revised Baltimore Catechism No. 1 (Confraternity), questions 81, 82, Text, p. 238.

2. Application:
Who really decides whether we should go to heaven or hell when we die? (We do.) How do you show God that you want to go to heaven? To hell? When should we start preparing for heaven? How? The children resolve to live every day as well as they can so they will be ready to welcome Jesus when He comes to judge them.

3. Organization:
   a) What happens to our bodies when we die?
   b) What happens to our souls?
   c) Which souls go to heaven?
   d) Which souls go to purgatory?
   e) Which souls go to hell?

4. Broader Organization:
Poem: "If I Should Die," Thayer, *The Child on His Knees*, p. 79.

5. Assignment:
Catechism questions 81 and 82, p. 238, at the end of Unit Six in children's text.
6. Suggested Activity:
The children draw pictures to illustrate the reward they expect after death.

UNIT SIX, PART 5 (cont.).

LESSON PLAN 153

The children read or reread and discuss Part 5, p. 227, in text.

UNIT SIX, PART 6, LESSON PLANS 154–157, The General Judgment. Text, p. 230.

LESSON PLAN 154

> "He will send forth his angels with a trumpet and a great sound" (Mt. 24:31).
> Blackboard

I. **SUBJECT MATTER**
General Judgment

II. **TYPE**
Development

III. **OBJECTIVES**
A. To give the children an understanding of general judgment.
B. To inspire the children to respect both their bodies and souls.
C. To lead the children to use their bodies and souls for good deeds.

IV. **MATERIALS**
Poem: "How God Will Reward Me," Sister Josita Belger, *Sing a Song of Holy Things,"* pp. 100–101.

V. **PROCEDURE**

A. Approach
We know that our bodies must die. Will they stay dead forever, or will they have a resurrection as our Lord's body had?

B. Presentation
1. Explanation and discussion:
   a) Explain vividly the destruction of the world and the resurrection of our bodies.
   b) Explain vividly the second coming of our Lord to judge the living and the dead.
      1) The appearance of our Lord.
      2) The gathering together of people.
      3) The separation of sheep (elect) from goats (damned).
      4) The sentence pronounced on each.
   c) Discuss the reason for this general judgment (define term) to show that our Lord is just by rewarding the good and punishing the bad.
   d) Explain that our bodies deserve to share in the rewards or punishments of our souls because we use our bodies to do good or evil while we are on earth; discuss ways in which our bodies will be different — glorious or hideous.
   e) Explain that Mary, by favor of her Assumption, will not have a resurrection of the body on the last day; discuss God's goodness in preserving His Mother's body from going back to dust.
   f) End the presentation by repeating exact answers of the Revised Baltimore Catechism, No. 1 (Confraternity), questions 78, 79, 80, 83, Text, pp. 237, 238.

2. Application:
Do you want to be a sheep or a goat on general resurrection day? The children resolve to love and obey God always so they can be sheep.

3. Organization:
Class composition:
   a) On the last day, the world will be destroyed by fire.
   b) The bodies of all men will rise from the grave.
   c) Jesus will come, sitting on the clouds in great majesty.
   d) Jesus will separate the sheep from the goats.
   e) Jesus will reward the sheep.
   f) He will punish the goats forever.

4. Broader Appreciation:
Poem: "How God Will Reward Me," Sister Josita Belger, *Sing a Song of Holy Things,* pp. 100–101.

5. Assignment:
Catechism questions 78, 79, 80, and 83, pp. 237, 238, at the end of Unit Six in children's text.

6. Suggested Activity:
The children write a report about what will happen at the end of the world.

UNIT SIX, PART 6 (cont.).

LESSON PLAN 155

The children read or reread and discuss Part 6, p. 230, in their text.

UNIT SIX, PART 6 (cont.).

LESSON PLAN 156

I. **SUBJECT MATTER**
The Holy Ghost and the Catholic Church

II. **TYPE**
Discussion

III. MATERIALS
Children's text, Unit Six, "Problem," p. 234.

IV. PROCEDURE
Same as for discussion plan, Unit One, Lesson 8, p. 13, in the Manual.

UNIT SIX, PART 6 (cont.).

LESSON PLAN 157

I. SUBJECT MATTER
God the Holy Ghost Comes to Do His Work

II. TYPE
Drill

III. MATERIALS
Questions at the end of Unit Six, p. 239, in children's text.

IV. PROCEDURE
Same as for drill lesson, Unit One, Lesson 21, p. 18, in the Manual.

III. Culmination of Unit Six

LESSON PLAN 158

I. SUBJECT MATTER
God the Holy Ghost Comes to Do His Work

II. TYPE
Culmination

III. MATERIALS
A. Hymns, poems, stories, etc., developed during this unit.

IV. PROCEDURE
Same as for culmination plan, Unit One, Lesson 22, p. 19, in Manual.

IV. Evaluation of Unit Six

LESSON PLAN 159

The children take the written test found at the end of Unit Six, pp. 239-240, in their text.

SPECIAL LESSONS FOR THE LITURGICAL YEAR (Unit Six)

*March 7 — St. Thomas Aquinas
  Prayer: "St. Thomas, patron of schools, pray for us."

March 17 — St. Patrick
  "St. Patrick, pray for us."

*March 19 — St. Joseph
  "St. Joseph, foster father of the Son of God, pray for us." *Litany of St. Joseph*

March 25 — The Annunciation
  "Hail Mary, full of grace," etc.

Holy Week, Easter Sunday

STUDY LESSON FOR THE FEAST OF ST. THOMAS AQUINAS

I. SUBJECT MATTER
Feast of St. Thomas Aquinas

II. TYPE
Development

III. OBJECTIVES
A. To give the children an understanding of and appreciation for the life and work of St. Thomas.
B. To lead the children to grow in love for Jesus in the Blessed Sacrament.

IV. MATERIALS
Poem: "In Church," Thayer, *The Child on His Knees*, pp. 12-13.

V. PROCEDURE

A. Approach
Discuss saint of today and the children's knowledge of this saint.

B. Presentation
1. Explanation and discussion:
   a) Tell briefly the story of the life of St. Thomas.
   b) Explain and discuss his titles and the reason for each:
      1) Saint of the Eucharist.
      2) Patron of Catholic Schools.
      3) Model of Students.
      4) Doctor of the Church.
2. Application:
   How do you know that St. Thomas loved Jesus in the Blessed Sacrament? The children resolve to show love for Jesus in the Blessed Sacrament by frequent visits and reception of Holy Communion.
3. Organization:
   List with children important facts in life of St. Thomas.
4. Broader Appreciation:
   Poem: "In Church," Thayer, *The Child on His Knees*, pp. 12, 13.
5. Suggested Activity:
   The children make up prayers suitable to be said before the Blessed Sacrament.

---

* *Feasts to be developed thoroughly; lesson plans have been worked out and will be found on the following pages.*

STUDY LESSON FOR THE FEAST OF ST. JOSEPH

I. SUBJECT MATTER
Feast of St. Joseph

II. TYPE
Development

III. OBJECTIVES
A. To bring the children to a better understanding and love of St. Joseph.

IV. MATERIALS
Poem: "The Joy of St. Joseph," Sister Josita Belger, *Sing a Song of Holy Things*, p. 53.

V. PROCEDURE

A. Approach
Does anyone know whose feast day is today?

B. Presentation
1. Explanation and discussion:
   a) Children discuss what they already know about St. Joseph.
   b) Explain that St. Joseph is the patron saint of many; give titles and explain each:
      1) Patron of the Church.
      2) Patron of the dying.
      3) Patron of the workingman.
2. Application:
   The children suggest ways in which they can honor St. Joseph today.
3. Organization:
   a) Who is St. Joseph?
   b) Why was he chosen to be the patron saint of the Church?
   c) Why is he the patron saint of the dying?
   d) Why is he the patron saint of the workingman?
4. Broader Appreciation:
   Poem: "The Joy of St. Joseph," Sister Josita Belger, *Sing a Song of Holy Things*, p. 53.
5. Suggested Activity:
   The children make scrapbooks which contain prayers to, pictures, poems, and stories of St. Joseph.

CORRELATED ACTIVITIES FOR UNIT SIX

Art
1. The children make a large frieze to illustrate the work of teaching, sanctifying, and ruling which the pope, bishops, and priests do.
2. The children study pictures of religious art from various countries to see how Catholics all over the world have the same beliefs.
3. The children make a large frieze to depict the last four things — death, judgment, heaven, hell.

Music
1. Hymns:
   a) Veni Creator, *St. Gregory Hymnal*, p. 199.
   b) Faith of Our Fathers, *St. Gregory Hymnal*, p. 121.
   c) Long Live the Pope, *St. Gregory Hymnal*, p. 122.

English
1. The children plan a home mission unit.
2. The children write letters to missionaries.
3. The children write original prayers, stories, poems, letters, reports, about topics of this unit.

Science
The children plan a unit on seeds and plants.

UNIT SEVEN. *HOW WE LOVE AND SERVE GOD*

(Text, *God's Truths Help Us Live*, pp. 241–280)

(Revised Baltimore Catechism No. 1 [Confraternity], Questions 84–105).

INTRODUCTORY MATERIAL

I. INTRODUCTION FOR THE TEACHER

The theme of this unit is a natural outgrowth of the year's study of the Creed. Through the study of the first three Commandments, the child discovers numerous ways of loving this great and good God so as to avoid offending Him. The Commandments, four to ten, on love of neighbor are only quickly reviewed to tie up the Commandments as a unit in the child's mind.

II. OBJECTIVES OF THE UNIT

A. To gain a better understanding of what the Commandments tell us to do and not to do in our relationship with God.
B. To realize the fact that knowledge of the Commandments will add to and strengthen our love of God.
C. To resolve to give God love for love in keeping His Commandments.
D. To realize that the Commandments established by God lead us to Him.

III. SUBJECT MATTER

A. We love and serve God by keeping His Commandments.
   1. The two great Commandments of Love.
   2. The first Commandment — what it commands and forbids.
   3. The second Commandment — what it commands and forbids.
   4. The third Commandment — what it commands and forbids.
   5. The last seven Commandments (brief review).

IV. TEACHER REFERENCES FOR UNIT SEVEN

1. Baierl, *The Commandments Explained*, pp. 40–173.
2. Belger, *Sing a Song of Holy Things*, pp. 37, 48, and 49.
3. Brennan, *Angel Food*, pp. 30–34, 74–75.
4. Brennan, *Going His Way*, pp. 70–73, 78–81, 91–94.
5. Johnson, *Bible Story*, pp. 94–98.
6. Lovasik, *Catechism Sketched*, pp. 50–61, 128–130.
7. Montani, *St. Gregory Hymnal*, pp. 26, 27, 39, 271, 274, 275.
8. Thayer, *The Child on His Knees*, pp. 27–78.

LESSON PLANS FOR UNIT SEVEN

I. Introduction to Unit Seven

How We Love and Serve God. Text, p. 241

LESSON PLAN 160

> "If you love Me, keep My Commandments" (Jn. 14:15).
>
> Blackboard

I. SUBJECT MATTER
The Ten Commandments

II. TYPE
Introduction

III. MATERIALS
Unit Seven, p. 241, in the children's text.

IV. PROCEDURE
Same as for introductory lesson — Unit Two, Lesson 24, p. 22, in the Manual.

II. Work Study Periods for Unit Seven
(Lesson Plans 161–184)

UNIT SEVEN, PART 1, The Law of Love. Text, p. 242

LESSON PLAN 161

> "By this shall all men know that you are My disciples, if you have love one for another" (Jn. 13:35).
>
> Blackboard

I. SUBJECT MATTER
The Law of Love

II. TYPE
Development

III. OBJECTIVES
A. To develop the understanding that the law of God is the law of love.
B. To develop the idea that we must love God, our neighbor, and ourselves.
C. To prove our love for God by keeping His Commandments.

IV. MATERIALS
Story: "A Piece of Glass," Brennan, *Going His Way,* pp. 78–81.

V. PROCEDURE

A. Approach

Discuss: Must we do more than believe God's truths if we want to go to heaven?

B. Presentation

1. Explanation and discussion:
   a) Explain that believing is not enough to save us — we must also keep God's law.
   b) Explain the law of love to the children. Discuss the two great Commandments that contain this whole law of love. Explain how they are divided and what God tells us to do in the first great Commandment — in the second great Commandment.
   c) Recall the incident in the life of Christ in which He gave the law of love.
   d) Explain that we love God, our neighbor, and ourselves by keeping the Ten Commandments. Recall the story of how God gave the Ten Commandments to Moses. Recall what the Ten Commandments are. Recall that the Commandments were written on two tablets of stone; explain how divided:
      1) The first three, written on one stone, tell us how to love God.
      2) The last seven, written on the other stone, tell us how to love our neighbor and ourselves; review term: neighbor.
   e) Explain that it will be easy to keep God's Commandments if we really love Him.
   f) End the presentation by repeating exact answers to the Revised Baltimore Catechism No. 1 (Confraternity), questions 84–87, Text, p. 273.
2. Application:
   Children suggest ways in which they can prove their love for God.
3. Organization:
   a) What must we do to love God, our neighbor, and ourselves?
   b) What do the first three Commandments tell us to do?
   c) What do the last seven tell us to do?
   d) Name the Ten Commandments.
4. Broader Appreciation:
   Story: "A Piece of Glass," Brennan, *Going His Way,* pp. 78–81.
5. Assignment:
   Study Catechism questions 84, 85, 86, and 87, p. 273, at the end of Unit Seven, in their text.
6. Suggested Activity:
   Make a list of stories from the Life of Christ which shows His kindness to others.

UNIT SEVEN, PART 1 (cont.).

LESSON PLAN 162

The children read or reread and discuss Part 1, p. 242, in their text.

UNIT SEVEN, PART 2, LESSON PLANS 163–166, The First Commandment and How We Keep It. Text, p. 246

LESSON PLAN 163

> "Have we not one Father? Has not one God created us?" (Mal. 2:10).
>
> Blackboard

I. SUBJECT MATTER
How We Keep the First Commandment

II. TYPE
Development

III. OBJECTIVES
A. To develop an understanding of the first Commandment.
B. To lead the children to the strong desire of keeping it.
C. To develop the attitude that we must worship God.

IV. MATERIALS
Story: "The Devil Is a Sissy," Brennan, *Angel Food,* pp. 74–75.

V. PROCEDURE

A. Approach

Recall the two great Commandments. Explain that today we will find out how we must love and serve God by keeping the first Commandment.

B. Presentation

1. Explanation and discussion:
   a) Explain and discuss what the first Commandment is and what it tells us to do: worship God alone. Define term: worship. Explain how we worship God and give examples:
      1) By faith:
         (a) By going to Mass.

            (b) By saying our daily prayers.
            (c) By genuflecting.
            (d) By not eating meat on Friday, etc.
        2) By hope:
            (a) By receiving the sacraments.
            (b) By trusting in God's help.
        3) By charity:
            (a) By telling God we love Him.
            (b) By doing God's will perfectly.
            (c) By loving our neighbor.
        4) By adoring Him; define term; give examples.
        5) By prayer; explain that we'll talk about prayer as a way to worship God in our next lesson.
      b) End the presentation by repeating exact answers to the Revised Baltimore Catechism, No. 1 (Confraternity), questions 88, 89, Text, p. 274.
   2. Application:
      The children suggest practices of worship for today.
   3. Organization:
      a) Whom must we worship?
      b) How do we worship God?
   4. Broader Appreciation:
      Story: "The Devil Is a Sissy," Brennan, *Angel Food*, pp. 74–75.
   5. Assignment:
      Study Catechism questions 88 and 89, p. 274, at the end of Unit Seven in their text.
   6. Suggested Activity:
      The children write the Acts of Faith, Hope, and Love.

UNIT SEVEN, PART 2 (cont.).

LESSON PLAN 164

> "You shall adore the Lord your God, and Him only shall you serve" (Lk. 4:8).
>
> Blackboard

I. SUBJECT MATTER
Prayer

II. TYPE
Development

III. OBJECTIVES
A. To develop the understanding of what prayer is.
B. To instill in the children right attitudes toward prayer.

IV. MATERIALS
Poem: "Little Prayer," Thayer, *Child on His Knees*, p. 27.

V. PROCEDURE

A. Approach
Discuss ways in which we love and serve God.

B. Presentation
1. Explanation and discussion:
   a) Discuss: What is prayer? Explain — it is the lifting up of our minds and hearts (wills) to God.
   b) Discuss why we pray; compare with four reasons why sacrifice is offered:
      1) Adore
      2) Thank
      3) Make up
      4) Ask
   c) Illustrate four types with brief stories of:
      1) The Publican
      2) Leper
      3) Prodigal Son
      4) St. Peter sinking
   d) Explain how we should pray:
      1) With exterior reverence
      2) With interior devotion
         Give examples.
   e) Discuss kinds of prayers to say:
      1) Those we know by heart.
      2) Those we can read in prayer books.
      3) Those said in our own words.
   f) Children tell personal experience in which prayers were answered.
   g) End presentation by repeating exact answer to the Revised Baltimore Catechism No. 1 (Confraternity), question 90, Text, p. 274.
2. Application:
   a) Children examine conscience:
      1) How do I pray?
      2) How often do I pray?
      3) How can I make my prayers better?
3. Organization:
   a) What is prayer?
   b) Why do we pray?
   c) How should we pray?
4. Broader Appreciation:
   Poem: "Little Prayer," Thayer, *Child on His Knees*, p. 27.
5. Assignment:
   Study Catechism question 90, p. 274, at the end of Unit Seven in their text.
6. Suggested Activities:
   The children find pictures of children at prayer.

UNIT SEVEN, PART 2 (cont.).

LESSON PLAN 165

> "For of Him, and by Him, and in Him are all things. To Him be glory forever" (Rom. 11:36).
>
> Blackboard

I. **SUBJECT MATTER**
Prayer

II. **TYPE**
Development

III. **OBJECTIVES**
A. To develop the understanding that we should pray to the angels and the saints.
B. To develop the attitude that we do not worship the saints and angels but honor them by our prayers.
C. To create an attitude that prayer is very necessary for salvation.

IV. **MATERIALS**
Poem: "For You," Thayer, *Child on His Knees*, p. 78.

V. **PROCEDURE**

A. **Approach**
Review the last discussion that we had on prayer.

B. **Presentation**
1. Explanation and discussion:
   a) Discuss to whom we should pray and why:
      1) Jesus
      2) Mary
      3) Angels
      4) Saints
   b) List special saints we should pray to and special grace we should ask from each.
   c) Discuss: For whom we should pray and what grace for each:
      1) Parents, relatives, friends
      2) Ourselves
      3) Enemies
      4) Poor Souls
      5) Rulers of the Church
      6) Anyone needing special prayers
   d) Show how to repay favors with prayers.
   e) Discuss: when should we pray:
      1) Morning, noon, night
      2) Before and after meals
      3) In church
      4) In danger
      5) In temptation
   f) Explain how necessary prayer is for salvation. Need to pray always — especially in the summertime.
   g) End the presentation by repeating exact answers of the Revised Baltimore Catechism No. 1 (Confraternity), questions 88, 89, 90, Text, p. 274.
2. Application:
   Make a resolution to pray for all — even those we do not know and at necessary times.
3. Organization:
   a) To whom should we pray?
   b) Name some saints to whom we should pray.
   c) For whom should we pray?
   d) When should we pray?
4. Broader Appreciation:
   Poem: "For You," Thayer, *Child on His Knees*, p. 78.
5. Assignment:
   Study Catechism questions 88, 89, and 90, p. 274, at the end of Unit Seven in children's text.
6. Suggested Activity:
   Children find stories of the saints in their readers and reread them.

UNIT SEVEN, PART 2 (cont.).

LESSON PLAN 166

The children read or reread and discuss Part 2, p. 246, in their text.

UNIT SEVEN, PART 3, The First Commandment and How We Break It. Text, p. 251

LESSON PLAN 167

> "Be faithful until death. And I will give you the crown of life" (Apoc. 2:10).
>
> Blackboard

I. **SUBJECT MATTER**
How We Break the First Commandment

II. **TYPE**
Development

III. **OBJECTIVES**
A. To develop the knowledge of how we break the first Commandment.
B. To acquire an appreciation and love of our prayers.

IV. **MATERIALS**
Story: "The Man Who Forgot God," Brennan, *Going His Way*, pp. 70–73.

V. **PROCEDURE**

A. **Approach**
Review what the first Commandment tells us to do. Worship God and honor the saints.

B. **Presentation**
1. Explanation and discussion:
   a) Explain what the first Commandment forbids (put on third grade level):
      1) Worshiping false gods; recall meaning of term: worship. Explain that we do not worship saints — we pray to them; explain

that we don't pray to statues or crucifixes; explain their use.
2) Neglecting to pray — daily prayers, etc. Compare neglect of food weakening the body with neglect of prayer weakening the soul.
3) Praying carelessly.
4) Sinning against the virtues of faith, hope, charity; recall meaning of each virtue.
   (a) Explain sins against faith:
      (1) Not believing God's truths.
      (2) Taking part in non-Catholic services.
   (b) Explain sins against hope:
      (1) Presumption
      (2) Despair
   (c) Explain sins against charity:
      (1) Hatred of God and neighbor
      (2) Sloth
      (3) Envy
      (4) Scandal
   (d) End the presentation by repeating exact answers to the Revised Baltimore Catechism No. 1 (Confraternity), questions 91–96, Text, pp. 275–276.
5) Abusing holy things — tell what to do with old religious articles.
6) Going to fortune tellers; wearing charms, etc.
2. Application:
Check daily prayers — say them? — how? How treat religious articles?
3. Organization:
In what ways can we break the first Commandment?
4. Broader Appreciation:
Story: "The Man Who Forgot God," Brennan, *Going His Way*, pp. 70–73.
5. Assignment:
Study Catechism questions 91, 92, 93, 94, 95, and 96, pp. 275–276, at the end of Unit Seven in their text.
6. Suggested Activity:
Have children make a list of all the religious articles they have at home.

UNIT SEVEN, PART 3 (cont.).

LESSON PLAN 168

The children read or reread and discuss Part 3, p. 251, in their text.

UNIT SEVEN, PART 3 (cont.).

LESSON PLAN 169

I. SUBJECT MATTER
The first Commandment

II. TYPE
Discussion

III. MATERIALS
Parts 2 and 3, pp. 246–255, in children's text.

IV. PROCEDURE
Same as for discussion plan, Unit One, Lesson 8, in the Manual.

UNIT SEVEN, PART 4, LESSON PLANS 170–171, The Second Commandment and How We Keep It. Text, p. 256

LESSON PLAN 170

> "Blessed be the Name of the Lord" (Ps. 112:2).
> Blackboard

I. SUBJECT MATTER
How We Keep the Second Commandment

II. TYPE
Development

III. OBJECTIVES
A. To give the children a knowledge of the second Commandment.
B. To develop love and reverence for the holy name of Jesus.

IV. MATERIALS
Poem: "The Holy Name of Jesus," Sister Josita Belger, *Sing a Song of Holy Things*, p. 37.

V. PROCEDURE

A. Approach
What is the second Commandment?

B. Presentation
1. Explanation and discussion:
   a) Explain words of second Commandment. Discuss various names of God and Jesus.
   b) Explain and discuss what the second Commandment tells us to do:
      1) Speak reverently about God, saints, holy things; give examples, discuss reasons for this reverence.
      2) Show reverence for God's holy name.
         (a) Discuss the phrase, "Hallowed be Thy Name."
         (b) Discuss the meaning and reason for the Divine Praises.
         (c) Discuss the power of God's name — tell about devils.
         (d) Discuss bowing of head at the name of Jesus.
   c) List with the children the times of the day

when they should say the holy name of Jesus; also any special times during their lives when they should say the Holy Name.
- d) Explain that holy people want to have the name of Jesus on their lips as they are dying; tell why.
- e) End the presentation by repeating exact answers to the Revised Baltimore Catechism No. 1 (Confraternity), questions 97, 98, Text, p. 276.
2. Application:
   - a) Say the holy name of Jesus with great reverence.
   - b) Bow your head at the name of Jesus.
   - c) Try to get the good habit of saying the name of Jesus many times during the day.
3. Organization:
   List times when we should say the name of Jesus.
4. Broader Appreciation:
   Poem: "The Holy Name of Jesus," Sister Josita Belger, *Sing a Song of Holy Things*, p. 37.
5. Assignment:
   Study Catechism questions 97 and 98, p. 276, at the end of Unit Seven in their text.
6. Suggested Activity:
   The children write a three-sentence story about some holy person they know.

UNIT SEVEN, PART 4 (cont.).

LESSON PLAN 171

The children read or reread and discuss Part 4, p. 256, in their text.

UNIT SEVEN, PART 5, LESSON PLANS 172–174, The Second Commandment and How We Break It. Text, p. 259

LESSON PLAN 172

> "Bless the Lord, O my soul, and let all that is within me bless His Holy Name" (Ps. 102:1).
>
> Blackboard

I. SUBJECT MATTER
How We Break the Second Commandment

II. TYPE
Development

III. OBJECTIVES
A. To develop the meaning of the words of the second Commandment.
B. To develop an attitude of reverence for God's Holy Name.

IV. MATERIALS
Story: "The Boy With the Nails," Brennan, *Angel Food*, pp. 30–34.

V. PROCEDURE

A. Approach
Review what the second Commandment tells us to do.

B. Presentation
1. Explanation and discussion:
   - a) Explain what the second Commandment forbids and give examples:
     1) Using God's name in anger or fun — profanity.
     2) Blasphemy — saying insulting things about God or making fun of holy persons and things; tell of King feasting with sacred vessels to show how God sometimes punishes this sin.
     3) Cursing — wishing evil on others.
        - (a) Discuss what we should do if playmates curse; how to break habit — say prayer.
        - (b) Since children confess sin of "swearing" at times, explain how to confess sins against second Commandment.
   - b) Explain that vulgar language is no sin, but good children won't use it — e.g., hell, damn, where the devil, etc.
   - c) End the presentation by repeating exact answers to the Revised Baltimore Catechism No. 1 (Confraternity), questions 99, 100, Text, p. 276.
2. Application:
   - a) Use language that God and others will be pleased to hear.
   - b) Whisper a prayer to make up for the sin of another.
   - c) Keep from getting others angry.
3. Organization:
   List ways in which we can break the second Commandment.
4. Broader Appreciation:
   Story: "The Boy With the Nails," Brennan, *Angel Food*, pp. 30–34.
5. Assignment:
   Study Catechism questions 99 and 100, p. 276, at the end of Unit Seven in their text.
6. Suggested Activity:
   The children find the Divine Praises in their prayer books and write them.

UNIT SEVEN, PART 5 (cont.).

LESSON PLAN 173

Children read or reread and discuss Part 5, p. 259, in their text.

UNIT SEVEN, PART 5 (cont.).

LESSON PLAN 174

I. SUBJECT MATTER
The Second Commandment

II. TYPE
Discussion

III. MATERIALS
Children's text, Parts 4 and 5, pp. 256–261.

IV. PROCEDURE
Same as for discussion plans, Unit One, Lesson 8 in the Manual.

UNIT SEVEN, PART 6, LESSON PLANS 175–176, The Third Commandment and How We Keep It. Text, p. 262

LESSON PLAN 175

> "Keep My Sabbath, for it is holy unto you" (Exod. 31:14).
>
> Blackboard

I. SUBJECT MATTER
How to Keep the Third Commandment

II. TYPE
Development

III. OBJECTIVES
A. To develop an understanding of what the third Commandment is and what it commands.
B. To instill in the children a love for God's day and the desire to keep it holy.

IV. MATERIALS
Story: "The First Sleeper," Brennan, *Going His Way*, pp. 91–94.

V. PROCEDURE

A. Approach
Recall how we keep the first Commandment. Explain that it is so important for us to worship God that He has put it in another Commandment.

B. Presentation
1. Explanation and discussion:
   a) Explain what the third Commandment is; define term: Lord's day.
   b) Explain what the third Commandment tells us to do: rest and keep God's day holy; explain reason for rest, reason for keeping one day of week holy.
   c) Explain and discuss how to keep God's day holy:
      1) By worshiping God on Sunday and the holydays by going to Mass; explain law of Church.
         (a) Discuss who must assist at Mass.
         (b) Discuss proper behavior at Mass.
         (c) Explain that whole Mass must be attended on Sunday or holyday.
         (d) Explain what to do if ill in bed on Sunday.
      2) By keeping Sunday as a day of prayer and good works.
         (a) Discuss pious practices for Sunday:
            (1) Making visits to the Blessed Sacrament or attending Benediction.
            (2) Saying the family rosary.
            (3) Visiting the sick or the cemetery.
            (4) Listening to Catholic programs.
            (5) Reading Catholic books, etc.
            (6) Saying extra prayers.
      d) End the presentation by repeating exact answers to the Revised Baltimore Catechism No. 1 (Confraternity), questions 101–103, Text, p. 277.
2. Application:
   The children make a resolution to go to Mass often and to assist well at every Mass.
3. Organization:
   a) What is the third Commandment?
   b) Why must we go to Mass on Sunday?
   c) How should we assist at Mass?
   d) What else can we do to keep Sunday holy?
4. Broader Appreciation:
   Story: "The First Sleeper," Brennan, *Going His Way*, pp. 91–94.
5. Assignment:
   Study Catechism questions 101, 102, and 103, p. 277, at the end of Unit Seven in their text.
6. Suggested Activity:
   Children make a survey of their homes to see if there are any Catholic books or magazines there.

UNIT SEVEN, PART 6 (cont.).

LESSON PLAN 176

The children read or reread and discuss Part 6, p. 262, in their text.

UNIT SEVEN, PART 7, LESSON PLANS 176–177, The Third Commandment and How We Break It. Text, p. 265.

LESSON PLAN 177

> "He blessed the seventh day and sanctified it" (Gen. 2:3).
>
> Blackboard

I. SUBJECT MATTER
How We Break the Third Commandment

II. TYPE
Development

III. OBJECTIVES
A. To further develop the understanding of the third Commandment and what it forbids.
B. To develop the attitude that Sunday is God's day and is a day of rest.

IV. MATERIALS
None

V. PROCEDURE

A. Approach
Recall how we keep Sunday holy.

B. Presentation
1. Explanation and discussion:
   a) Explain what the third Commandment forbids.
      1) Missing Mass on Sunday without a good reason; stress gravity of sin.
      2) Being late for Mass on Sunday; explain what to do if we miss an important part of Mass.
      3) Doing unnecessary servile work; explain term; servile work.
   b) List things we can do and cannot do on Sunday.
   c) Discuss neighborhood observance of Sunday.
   d) End the presentation by repeating exact answers of the Revised Baltimore Catechism No. 1 (Confraternity), questions 104, 105, Text, p. 277.
2. Application:
   Children resolve to keep Sunday holy; never to miss Mass on Sunday without a good reason; and to be on time for Mass.
3. Organization:
   What does the third Commandment forbid?
4. Broader Application:
   The children make up a prayer to God promising to do all they can to keep Sunday holy.
5. Assignment:
   Study Catechism questions 104 and 105, p. 277, at the end of Unit Seven in their text.
6. Suggested Activity:
   Children make a picture book to show how to keep Sunday holy.

UNIT SEVEN, PART 7 (cont.).

LESSON PLAN 178

Children read or reread and discuss Part 7, p. 265, in their text.

UNIT SEVEN, PART 8, LESSON PLANS 179–182, The Last Seven Commandments of God. Text, p. 268.

LESSON PLAN 179

> "Amen I say to you, as long as you did it for one of these, the least of my brethren, you did it for me" (Mt. 31:40).
>
> Blackboard

I. SUBJECT MATTER
The Last Seven Commandments

II. TYPE
Development

III. OBJECTIVES
A. To develop an understanding of the last seven Commandments.
B. To instill a deeper love for our neighbor out of love for God.

IV. MATERIALS
Poem: "My Neighbor," Sister Josita Belger, *Sing a Song of Holy Things*, pp. 48–49.

V. PROCEDURE

A. Approach
Recall how we can love and serve God by loving our neighbor.

B. Presentation
1. Explanation and discussion:
   a) Explain that we love our neighbor by keeping the last seven Commandments.
   b) Explain briefly what each of the last seven Commandments tells us to do:
      1) Fourth Commandment — obey.
      2) Fifth Commandment — be kind and patient.
      3) Sixth Commandment — be pure.
      4) Seventh Commandment — do not steal.
      5) Eighth Commandment — tell the truth.
      6) Ninth Commandment — have pure thoughts.
      7) Tenth Commandment — do not want other children's things.
   c) Give examples of how we keep and break each of these Commandments.
   d) List with children kind and unkind actions to our neighbor — things we want or don't want done to us.
   e) Discuss the necessity of last seven Commandments from the viewpoint of the Last Judgment.
2. Application:
   What can we do for our neighbor to show our love for God?

3. Organization:
   a) What does the fourth Commandment tell us to do?
   b) What does the fifth Commandment tell us to do?
   c) What do the sixth and ninth Commandments tell us to do?
   d) What do the seventh and tenth Commandments tell us to do?
   e) What does the eighth Commandment tell us to do?
4. Broader Appreciation:
   Poem: "My Neighbor," Sister Josita Belger, *Sing a Song of Holy Things*, pp. 48–49.
5. Assignment:
   None
6. Suggested Activity:
   Children compose a prayer in which they ask God to help them keep the Ten Commandments well.

UNIT SEVEN, PART 8 (cont.).

LESSON PLAN 180

Children read or reread and discuss, Part 8, p. 268, in their text.

UNIT SEVEN, PART 8 (cont.).

LESSON PLAN 181

I. SUBJECT MATTER
The Ten Commandments — "Problems"

II. TYPE
Discussion

III. MATERIALS
Children's text, "Problems," at the end of Unit Seven, pp. 271–272 in text.

IV. PROCEDURE
Same as for discussion plan, Unit One, Lesson 8, p. 13, in the Manual.

UNIT SEVEN, PART 8 (cont.).

LESSON PLAN 182

I. SUBJECT MATTER
The Ten Commandments

II. TYPE
Drill

III. MATERIALS
Questions at the end of Unit Seven, p. 278 in the children's text.

IV. PROCEDURE
Same as for drill lesson, Unit One, Lesson 21, p. 18, in the Manual.

III. Culmination of Unit Seven

LESSON PLAN 183

I. SUBJECT MATTER
The Ten Commandments

II. TYPE
Culmination

III. MATERIALS
  A. Hymns, poems, stories, etc., developed during this unit.

IV. PROCEDURE
Same as for culmination plan, Unit One, Lesson 22, p. 19, in the Manual.

IV. Evaluation of Unit Seven

LESSON PLAN 184

The children take the written test, pp. 279–280, found in their text at the end of Unit Seven.

SPECIAL LESSONS FOR THE LITURGICAL YEAR (Unit Seven)

April 30 — St. Catherine of Siena
"O God, Thou art all powerful, make me a Saint." (*Raccolta*, 15)

May — Month of Mary
"My Queen! my Mother! I give thee all myself, and, to show my devotion to thee, I consecrate to thee my eyes, my ears, my mouth, my heart, my entire self. Wherefore, O loving Mother, as I am thine own, keep me, defend me, as thy property and possession." (*Raccolta*, 340)

Ascension Day
"Lord, increase our faith." (*Raccolta*, 38)

Pentecost
"Come Holy Spirit, fill the hearts of Thy faithful and kindle in them the fire of Thy love." (*Raccolta*, 287)

Trinity Sunday
"I believe in Thee, I hope in Thee, I love Thee, I adore Thee, O Blessed Trinity, one God." (*Raccolta*, 40)

Corpus Christi
"O Jesus in the Blessed Sacrament, have mercy on us." (*Raccolta*, 134)

CORRELATED ACTIVITIES FOR UNIT SEVEN

Art
1. The children start a class notebook to illustrate the positive and negative aspect of each of the Ten Commandments.
2. The children make symbols of faith, hope, and charity.
3. The children make a large frieze of some of the saints.
4. The children may set up the name of Jesus in design.
5. The children make a movie of a family spending a Sunday in the correct way.

Music
Hymns:
1. Kyrie Eleison, Sanctus, Benedictus, Agnus Dei, *St. Gregory Hymnal*, pp. 271, 274, 275.
2. All Glory, Laud and Honor, *St. Gregory Hymnal*, pp. 26, 27.
3. Holy God, We Praise Thy Name, *St. Gregory Hymnal*, p. 39.

English
1. The children dramatize any story taken in this unit.
2. The children memorize any poems taken in this unit.
3. The children write original prayers, letters, or stories about topics in this unit.

Science
The children talk about animals and plants living according to God's law. Lead the children to realize that plants and animals (also nonliving) must obey God's laws.

Lightning Source UK Ltd.
Milton Keynes UK
UKHW05f1426151018
330578UK00005B/110/P